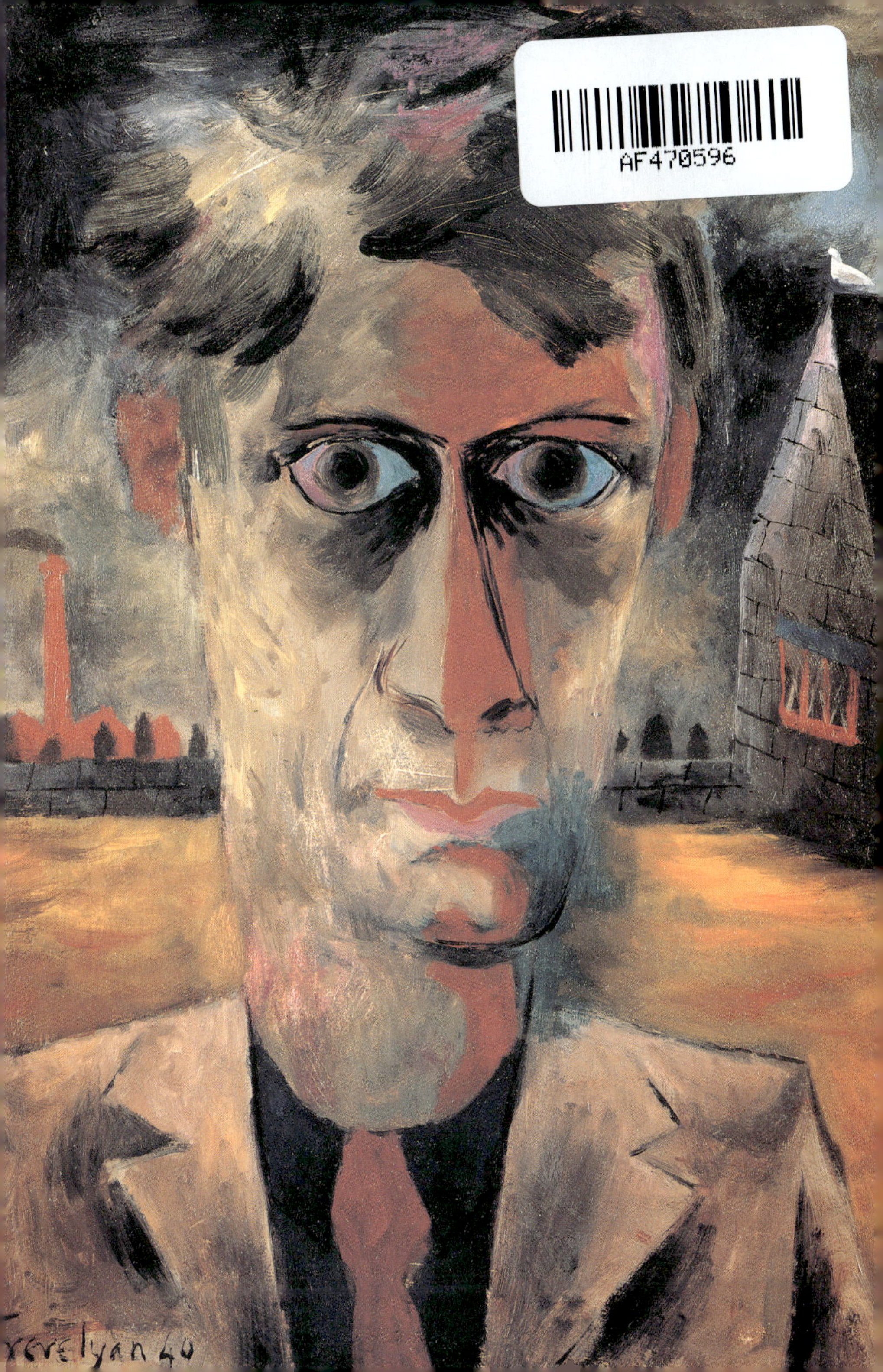
AF470596
Trevelyan 40

Self-portraits

Published in Great Britain by National Portrait Gallery Publications, National Portrait Gallery, St Martin's Place, London WC2H 0HE

For a complete catalogue of current publications please write to the address above, or visit our website at www.npg.org.uk/publications

ISBN 13: 978-1-85514-363-0
ISBN 10: 1-85514-363-1

A catalogue record for this book is available from the British Library.

Publishing Manager: Celia Joicey
Editorial consultant: Robin Gibson
Editor: Susie Foster
Design: Pentagram
Production: Ruth Müller-Wirth and Geoff Barlow
Printed and bound in Hong Kong

National Portrait Gallery
Insights

Self-portraits
Liz Rideal

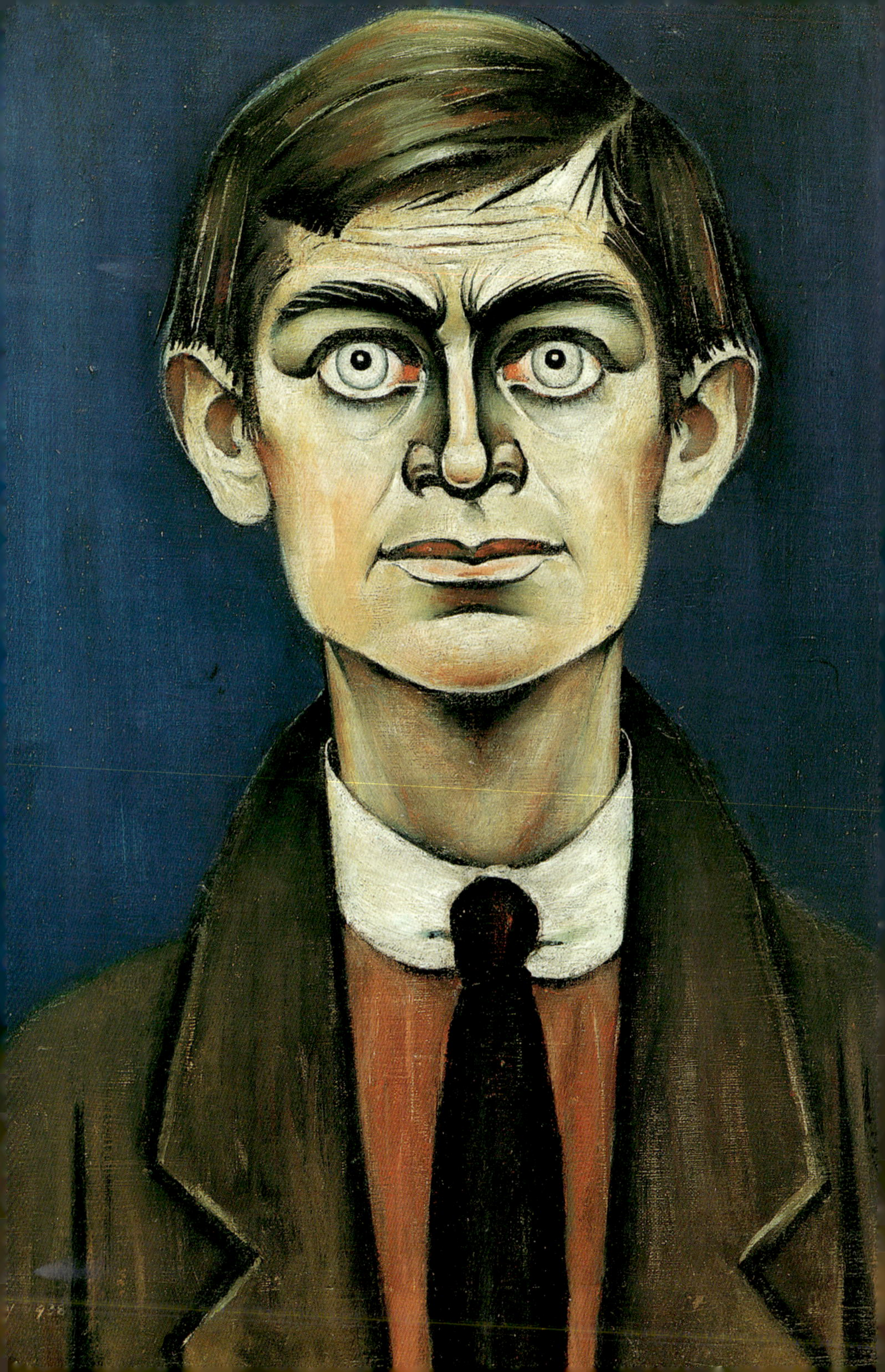

Contents

L.S. (Laurence Stephen) Lowry (1887–1976), 1938

Lowry attended Manchester and Salford Schools of Art. He spent his whole life in England, working for a rent-collecting company for forty-two years. This self-portrait is similar to several other portraits from the late 1930s, each with a full-frontal pose, staring red-rimmed eyes and plain backdrop. Lowry commented 'All the paintings of that period were done under stress and tension and they were all based on myself.'

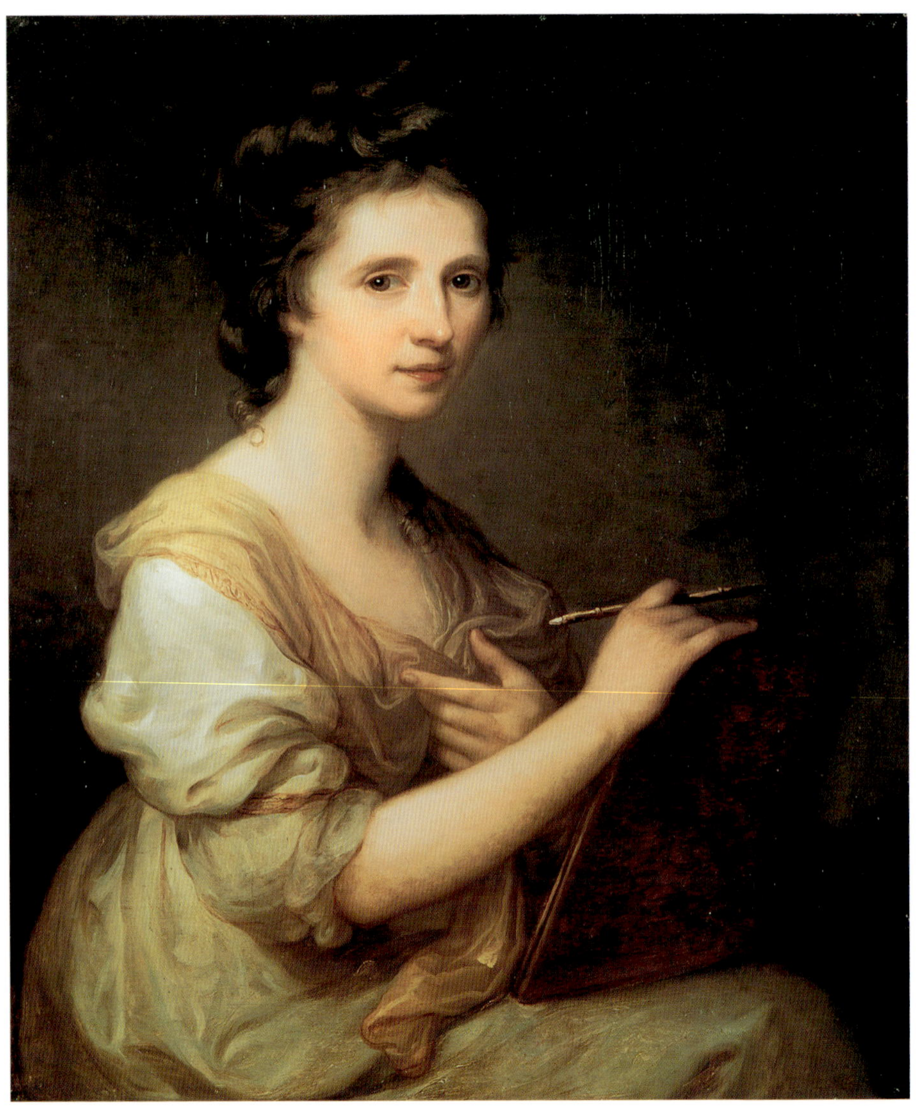

Introduction

The self-portrait is the artist's most personal form of expression. It is the ultimate means of self-analysis, presenting an opportunity for self-reflection, self-expression and self-promotion; a bid for eternity. One of art's most fascinating subjects, the self-portrait often repeats familiar conventions in portraiture but it also brings scope for complex interpretation.

The first collection of self-portraits was begun in the mid-seventeenth century by Cardinal Leopoldo de' Medici (1617–75) and is now housed in the Vasari Corridor at the Uffizi Gallery, Florence. The artists represented in this collection include not only Vasari – the architect of the Corridor – but also Dürer, Raphael, Rubens, Rembrandt, Velázquez, David, Delacroix and Ensor. Women artists featured include Anguissola, Kauffmann and Vigée-Lebrun.

Self-portraiture is a powerful means to ensure artistic survival and art historical recognition. But a self-portrait may sometimes also be cryptic or concealed, recognisable only to friends and cognoscenti. Examples of this are Lorenzo Ghiberti's self-portrait, which he included on the bronze doors of the Florence Baptistry in the early fifteenth century, and Michelangelo's painting of himself in the guise of the flayed skin of St Bartholomew in the Sistine Chapel. The notion that 'every painter paints himself' (*ogni dipintore dipinge se*) was part of artistic thinking in Renaissance Italy. The Italian polemicist Girolamo Savonarola (1452–98) believed that 'each work of art automatically reveals its author's hand and spiritual state', what we might now term the artist's stylistic signature. Leonardo da Vinci (1452–1519) went further than Savonarola, arguing in his writings that this urge to paint the self is an artist's greatest defect.

Commissioned self-portraits are rare and are normally made for patrons who admire the artist, and

Angelica Kauffmann
(1741–1807), *c.*1770–75

Born in Switzerland, Angelica Kauffmann was a child prodigy who painted her first self-portrait, with music score, aged thirteen. She was a founder member of the Royal Academy of Arts, London, and in 1787 was commissioned to produce a self-portrait for the prestigious Vasari Corridor in the Uffizi Gallery, Florence. The resulting work is similar to this self-portrait in that she is also dressed in white and holds a porte-crayon in her right hand, as if in the act of drawing.

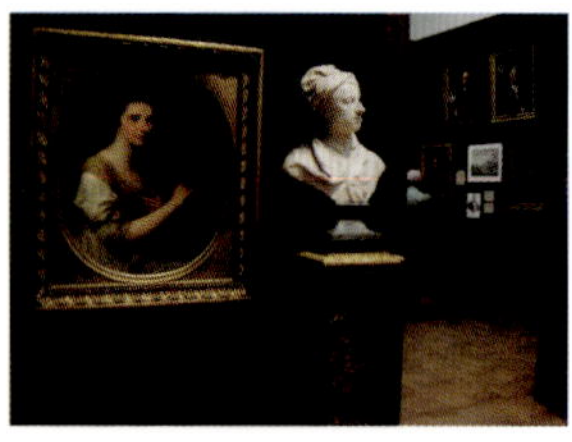

View of the 18th Century Galleries at the National Portrait Gallery, London

Angelica Kauffmann's self-portrait hangs alongside that of the architect Isaac Ware (1707?–66), c.1741, sculpted in marble after Louis-François Roubiliac.

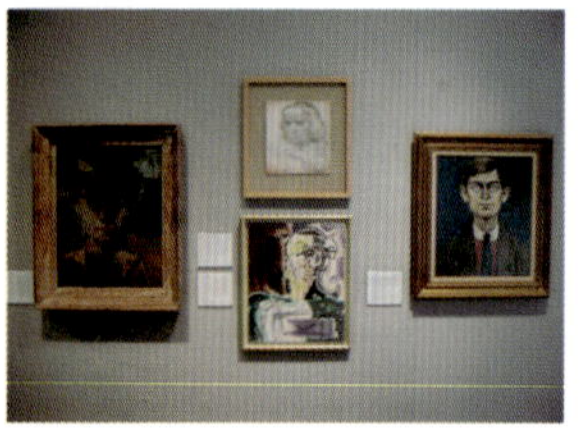

View of the 20th Century Galleries at the National Portrait Gallery, London

Patrick Heron's self-portrait of 1951 contrasts in style with the self-portraits of Julian Trevelyan (page 21), Barbara Hepworth (page 99) and L.S. Lowry (page 4).

want to record their association, or for dealers and investors in art who see the financial potential of commissioning an artist's image for their collection. In most instances, however, the artist chooses to create a self-portrait and to have complete control over its production. The artist is his or her own free model: according to the French painter Henri Fantin-Latour (1836–1904), an avid self-portraitist, 'The model is always ready and offers all sorts of advantages, he is exact, submissive and one knows him before painting!' This flexibility is liberating, but also complicated as the possibilities for self-representation are endless.

The production of a self-portrait is often a rite of passage for a young artist but because artists are aware of its potential legacy, it can be a daunting undertaking. Combining the urge to create with the desire to achieve something worthwhile means that artists frequently look to the work of others, often experiencing the difficulties of placing themselves simultaneously in both a contemporary and historic context. George Frederic Watts and Glyn Philpot, for instance, pay homage to the technique and composition of Titian and Diego Velázquez in their respective self-portraits (see pages 12 and 68). Helen Chadwick's self-portrait of 1986 refers to Jan Lys's painting *Vanitas* from the mid-seventeenth century, which personifies the female vice of vanity (page 17), and Richard Cosway in his self-portrait of 1770, wears Van Dyck dress (page 92).

Self-portraiture records not only what artists look like but also how they interpret themselves and the world around them. Gustave Courbet's *The Painter's Studio* (subtitled *A true allegory concerning seven years of my artistic life*, 1855; Musée d'Orsay, Paris) is an expanded view of this. Courbet (1819–77), the realist, formalises his portrait, making his context the microcosm of his own life: the model, the friends and patrons, the studio and his vision on the easel. By comparison, the Dutch

Introduction

Sir Joshua Reynolds
(1723–92), *c*.1747–9

Reynolds was the first President
of the Royal Academy of Arts.
His annual 'Discourse' to the
students outlined his painting
theories. In this portrait he holds
a shovel palette and maulstick in
his left hand, while shading
his eyes with his right, thereby
focusing our attention on his
most precious painting tools,
his hands and eyes.

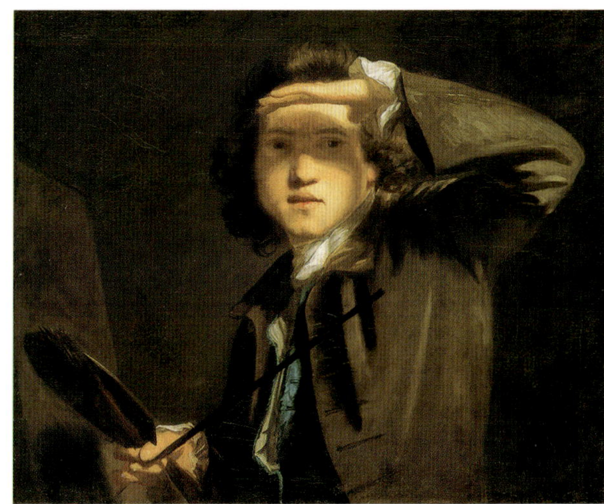

artist Edward Collier (page 15) offers a calm, modest
view of his life and studio, while John Bratby (page
18), with his vigorous impasto, presents himself self-
confidently, indeed twice over, in a studio that is
bright, brash and bold.

Self-perception is a curious thing. Over the years,
our emotions and experiences ricochet round inside
our heads, gradually emerging in our patterns of
behaviour and in our faces. Brimming with confidence
or shuddering with insecurity, artists are no different.
The self-portraits selected to illustrate this book show
them in many guises. Some emphasise the artist's
professional status by featuring palettes, easels, brushes
and cameras, others indicate success by focusing on
clothing and interiors, and some emphasise a mood or
emotion through disguise, pose, gesture or expression.

All of the self-portraits in this book are from the
collections of the National Portrait Gallery in London.
The first self-portrait to enter the Gallery in 1858 was
that of the artist and founder of the Royal Academy,
Sir Joshua Reynolds (1723–92) painted in *c*.1747–9.
However the earliest self-portrait in the collection is of

Self-portraits

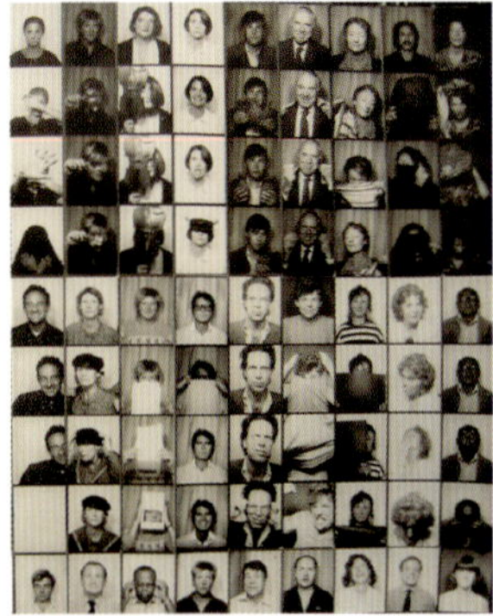

Identity (detail)
Liz Rideal (b.1954), 1985

Since the 1930s, the photo-booth has been pivotal in the mass-production of identity images. These tiny pictures are synonymous with the communality of everyday life, while at the same time defining the precious distinction of the individual, harking back to the carte-de-visite and before that to miniature painting. *Identity* is a mass self-portrait work consisting of 1,220 photographic strips that include 4,880 individual self-portraits, featuring artists such as Tony Bevan, Helen Chadwick and Maggi Hambling, to make up the larger self-portrait of Liz Rideal.

Gerlach Flicke (*fl.*1545; d.1558), painted in 1554, but only acquired in 1996 (see page 46). New acquisitions are made every year and there are now over 725 artists' self-portraits in the collection. Within the Gallery the proportion of men to women is high, and the number of ethnic minority artists is small, reflecting the history and prejudices of our society. Time and an evolving acquisitions policy are helping to redress the balance.

The collection is particularly strong in early twentieth-century self-portraits, reflecting the increasing opportunities for artists and aesthetic developments abroad. Contemporary technologies have broadened the definition of what self-portaiture can be. In the 1960s, the American artist Robert Morris (b.1931) was working on ideas based on conceptual portraiture, using bottled body fluids and medical scans. Mona Hatoum produced *Corps Etranger* in 1994, a video installation of an endoscopic journey through the landscape of her own body, and Marc Quinn's cryogenic sculpture *Self* (1997) contains nine pints of his own blood.

The self-portrait offers artists an opportunity to advertise their skills to prospective patrons. The development of the print process enabled the reproduction of such images, and the subsequent invention of photography has further facilitated the ability of artists past and present to enhance their reputations. The fact that artists make repeated observations over a lifetime means that for some, self-portraits may begin to construct a visual autobiography. The diversity of results and the gradual maturation of such work can lead to a valuable record of innovation: Edvard Munch (1863–1944), for example, produced seventy-two self-portraits in his lifetime, which mirror his ongoing self-questioning (some might say lapses into insanity). Madame Yevonde (see pages 74–5) and Jonathan

Introduction

Dame Ethel Walker
(1861–1951), *c*.1925

Walker's self-portrait attests
her commitment to Impressionist
technique. She studied at the
Slade School of Art and
attended Walter Sickert's
evening classes. In 1900 she
was the first woman painter to
be elected to the New English
Art Club and she represented
Britain twice in the Venice
Biennale, in 1930 and 1932.

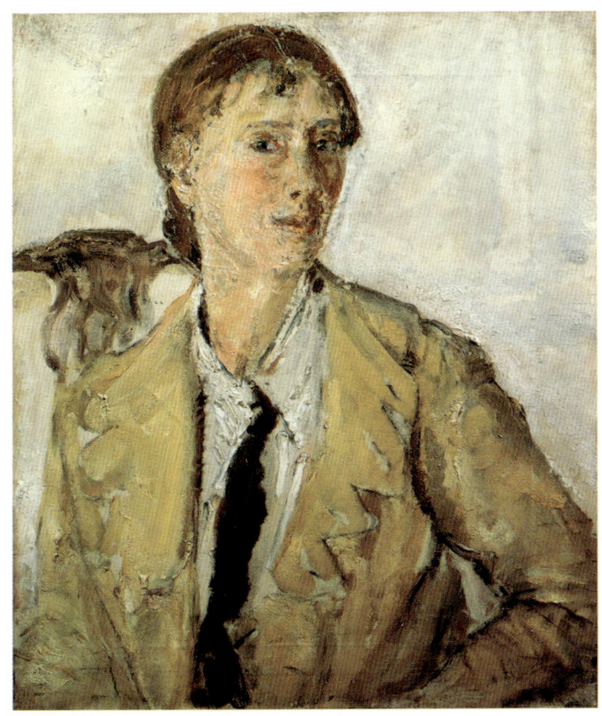

Richardson (page 66) also record their gradual
physical decay, giving an objective portrayal of the
ageing process.

Artists today have found a renewed relevance in
the complexity of self-portraiture: the memento mori
aspect of the genre is particularly pertinent in an age
of iris recognition, DNA and animal cloning. Proof
of identity is also of increasing importance to Western
society. As populations shift and our world becomes
increasingly globalised, self-imagery can take on a new
significance for the artist. Making a self-portrait is a
powerful tool for proclaiming the artists's physical and
cultural identity.

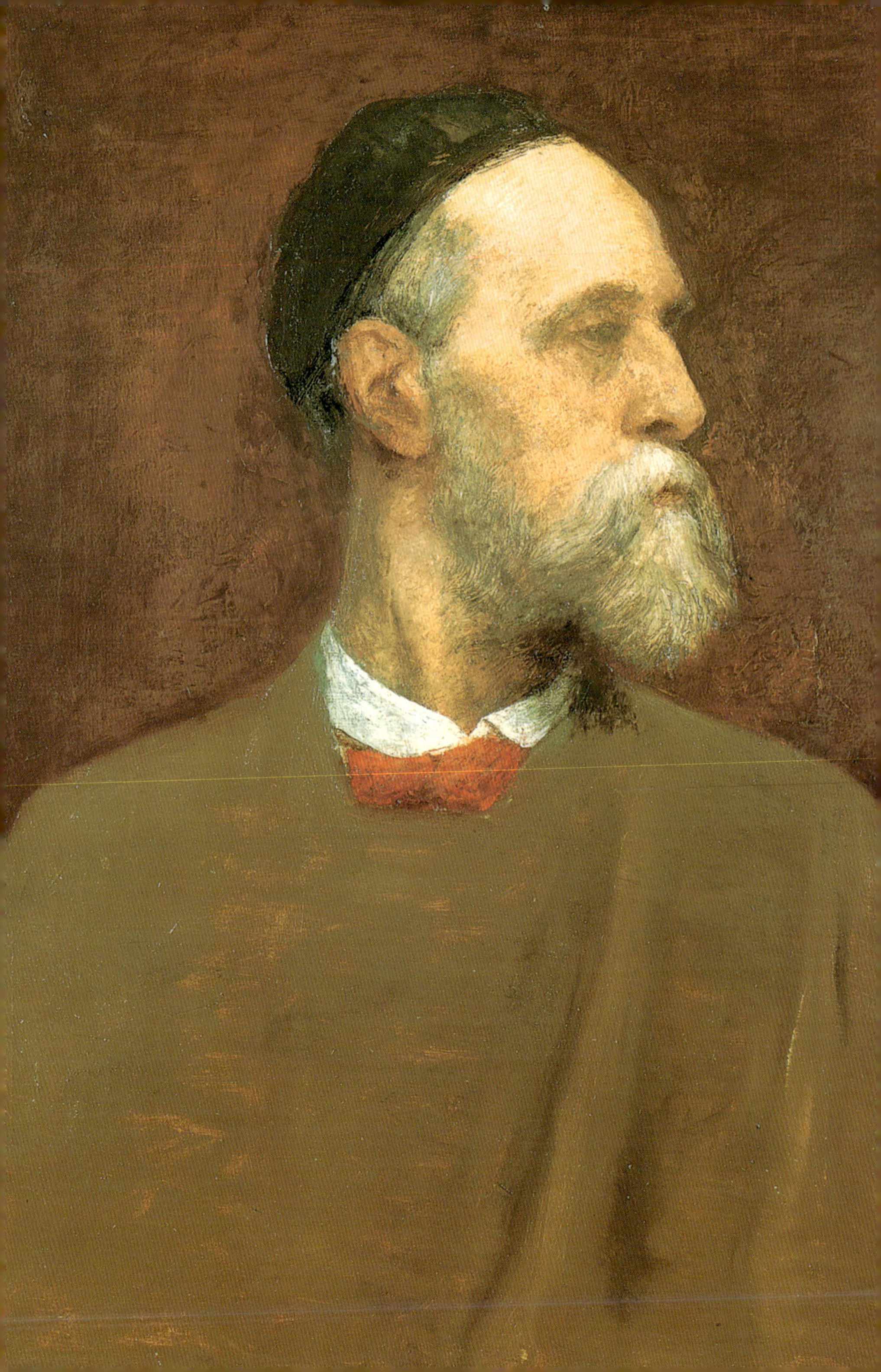

Chapter one
Vanitas: self-promotion and mortality

Vanity, self-interest and self-promotion are all key reasons why artists choose to paint or record their own image. The Latin word *vanitas* however is also the name given to a genre of still-life painting that became fashionable in the Netherlands in the sixteenth century after the Reformation. This genre was derived in part from the 'Dance of Death' woodcuts of the fifteenth century, which showed people from all walks of life in dialogue with Death portrayed as a skeleton. Such still-life paintings dwelt on the fragility of life, with symbols such as skulls, butterflies and guttering candles representing the transience of earthly achievements and pleasures. Ironically, the purchase of these paintings by wealthy clients was testament to their own worldly riches.

The term 'memento mori' can also be applied to paintings of the Vanitas genre: it is derived from the Latin meaning 'remember you must die'. In his signed painting *Still Life* (1699; Tate, London), Edward Collier (*fl.*1673–1706) includes the aphorism *'Vita Brevis, Ars Longa'* (life is short, art endures), and on a *trompe l'œil* piece of paper repeats his signature, 'Mr. E. Collier Painter at London'. He specifically uses text to underline his artistic position and affirm the enduring nature of his art.

Some of the self-portraits illustrated in this chapter adopt various aspects of the traditional Vanitas painting in their treatment of the theme of the inevitability of death by their inclusion of temporal objects, but others simply illustrate the artist's desire to be included in the annals of history. In his *Portrait of a Man* (1433; National Gallery, London), believed to be his self-portrait, Jan van Eyck (1385–1440) painted the words *'Als Ich Kan'* (As [well as] I can) onto the original frame. The *'Ich'* here puns with his name,

George Frederic Watts
(1817–1904), *c.*1879

Watts made three late self-portraits based on that of the Renaissance artist Titian, painted when Titian was in his late seventies, in profile and wearing a skull cap (Prado, Madrid). Watts solidifies his artistic credentials by aligning himself with the master, but simultaneously reveals his ambition for artistic longevity. Edward Steichen (1879–1973) reiterated this pose in his photograph of Watts taken during Steichen's European visit of 1902 to 1903.

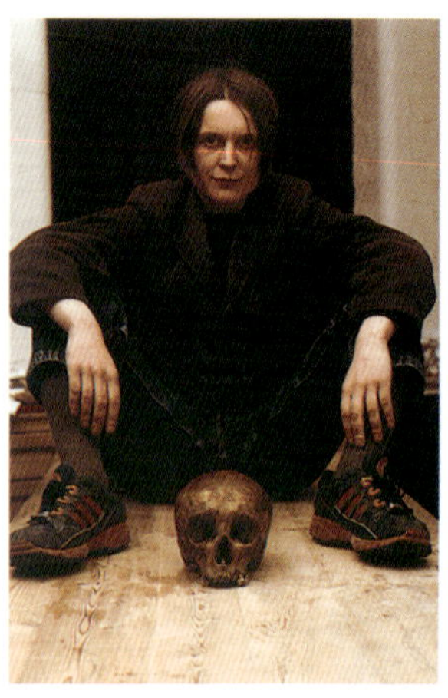

Self-portrait with Skull
Sarah Lucas (b.1962), 1997

This is one of twelve stridently 'unfeminine' photographic prints gifted to the National Portrait Gallery. Lucas appears in different guises: a fish slung over her shoulder, obscured by beer froth, in front of a line of knickers, crouching on a lavatory pan and, in this example, seated with a skull. The results seem designed to gain attention with their vaguely grubby, partly sexual innuendo. The emphasis seems more on a lack of vanity (she wears jeans and trainers), but there is a simultaneous awareness of Vanitas – particularly here with the traditional skull, but also with props like the dead fish.

Eyck. In his *Portrait of Giovanni Arnolfini and his Wife* (1434; National Gallery, London) Van Eyck incorporates the words '*Johannes de Eyck fuit hic* [was here]'. He catches his reflection in the central spherical convex mirror, taking centre stage for eternity. George Frederic Watts was also inclined to make a bid for immortality. Known as 'Signor' and dubbed 'England's Michaelangelo' by some of his contemporaries, he cast himself in the role of a modern old master.

The 1860s saw a tremendous enthusiasm for exploiting photography and translating painterly ideas into the new medium. David Wilkie Wynfield, for example, broadened the Victorian exploration of the genre by reviving the tradition of portraying sitters in fancy dress in his photographs (see his self-portrait on page 94). Richard Cockle Lucas (page 34) was another avid exponent of the new fashion for, and possibilities of, photography in the nineteenth century.

Helen Chadwick self-consciously styled her self-portrait *Vanitas II* in the manner of a Vanitas painting from the past (page 17). This photograph was taken at the Institute of Contemporary Arts, London, in 1986 on the occasion of Chadwick's solo exhibition *Of Mutability*. In 1952, John Minton commissioned Lucian Freud to paint his portrait, which was bequeathed after his suicide five years later to the Royal College of Art. When Freud learnt of this bequest he is said to have been convinced that Minton must have commissioned it with his death already in mind. Minton's self-portrait, painted soon afterwards, is like a mirror image of Freud's and possesses the same ghostly feel. In both portraits Minton's taut, angular features and baleful eyes dominate. Like Chadwick, he seems in retrospect an intense, elfin presence whose life was cut tragically short.

Altogether more upbeat is John Bratby who updates the genre by including studio paraphernalia

Vanitas: self-promotion and mortality

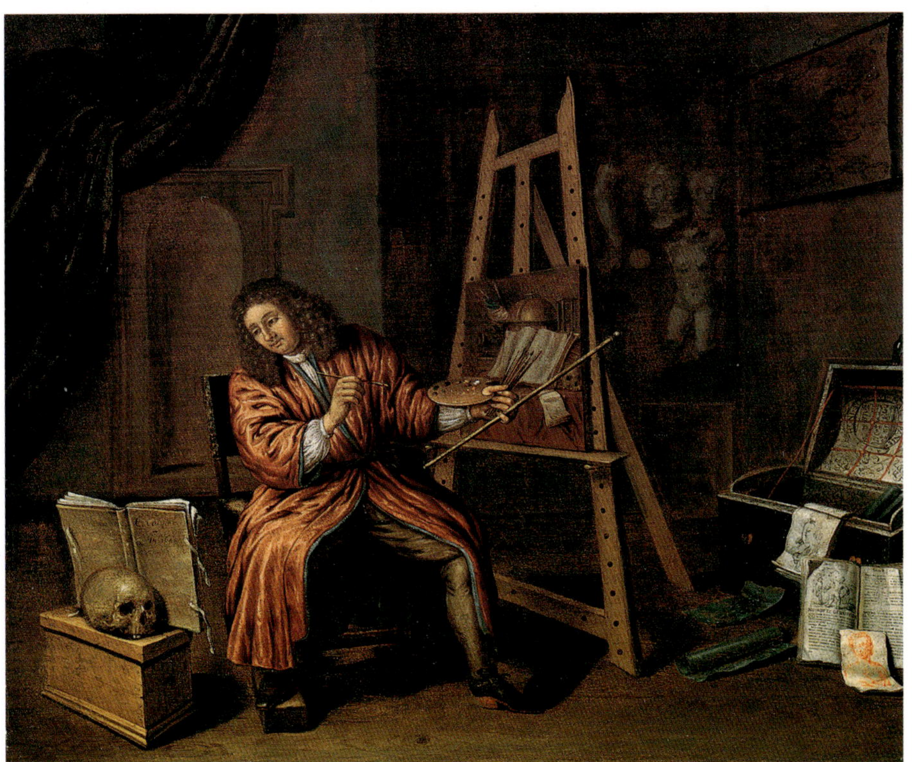

Edward Collier
(fl.1673–1706), 1683

This delightful small oil depicts Edward Collier alone in his studio, sporting an informal silken gown. He came to England in 1693, specialising in covetable still-life *trompe l'œil* paintings. Here he invites us to visit his realm and view his collection of props: a skull, a chest, drawings, sculpture and books, items that he would have recycled in his works. Objects such as these remind us of the transience of life, and are familiar symbols in Vanitas painting.

and contemporary clothing. He depicts himself life-size, both front and back, on a canvas over two metres tall, revelling in the super-thick, trowelled-on paint that had become his trademark. Ten years earlier, Bratby had produced sets and paintings for the film *The Horse's Mouth*, Joyce Cary's story of maverick painter Gulley Jimpson. This made Bratby famous: in a curious way the film, with Bratby's paintings, some of which are literally bulldozed on screen, is another interpretation of the notion of an enduring artistic Vanitas.

Self-portraits

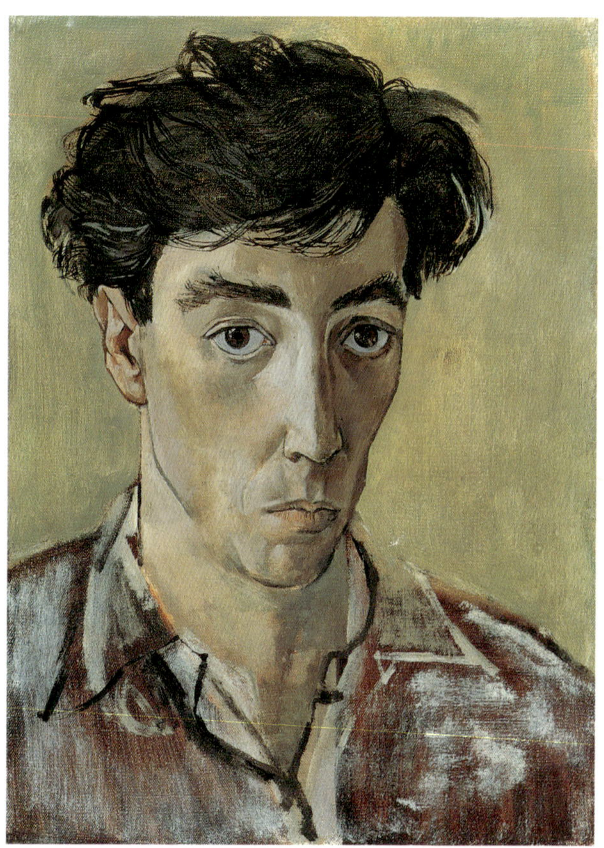

John Minton
(1917–57), *c*.1953

John Minton was a member of the Soho set, a group of artists so
called because they frequented Soho drinking clubs such as the
Colony Room. He was a major figure in the Neo-Romantic movement
of the 1940s and 1950s. He committed suicide at the age of thirty-
nine and this portrait conveys the deeply melancholic side to his
character. However, in life he had a reputation for being a generous
and vital personality. 'No-one,' he wrote, 'mirrors his age clearer
than the artist. For here is the living moment made concrete, the
particular made general, the symptoms diagnosed, the order made
from disorder.'

Vanitas: self-promotion and mortality

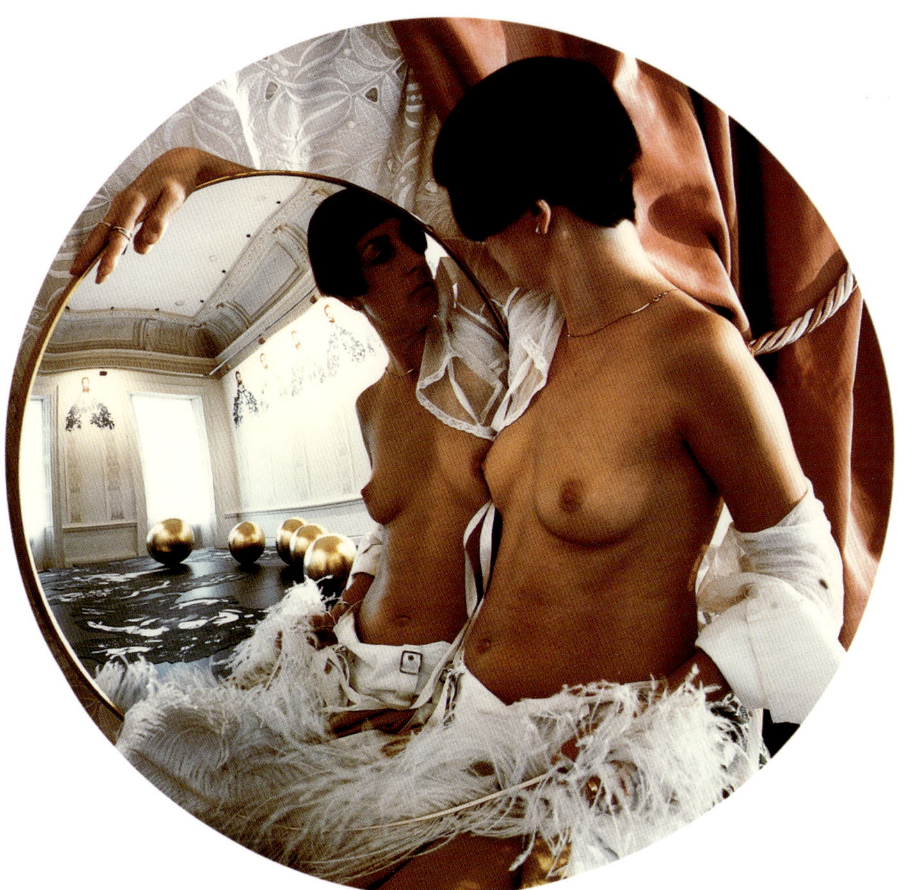

Vanitas II
Helen Chadwick (1953–96), 1986

Typically provocative, Chadwick combines feathers and bare breasts,
multiplied in the mirror for good measure. The golden balls pointedly
reflect her humour, being based on the size ratio of fingers – a covert
reference to the hand of the artist. The walls of the ICA gallery are
hung with computer-generated printouts and the blue photocopies
beneath the golden balls record her performance as protagonist in a
series of fantastic scenarios. As an artist, part of her strength lay in her
eagerness to innovate and her cleverness in responding to new
technical possibilities.

Self-portraits

John Bratby
(1928–92), 1967

Concentrating on the raw basics of human life, Bratby's choice of subject matter ranged from images of the lavatory to the breakfast table. As with many self-portraits, what appears to be a traditional, timeless work actually locates him firmly in his own timeframe: his leather jerkin, heavy framed glasses and the model's pointed shoes are typical of the 1960s. These objects, combined with the disarray of his painting equipment, indicate an admission of the temporary nature of our lives. Including himself twice also somehow seems to suggest the urgency of capturing the passing moment.

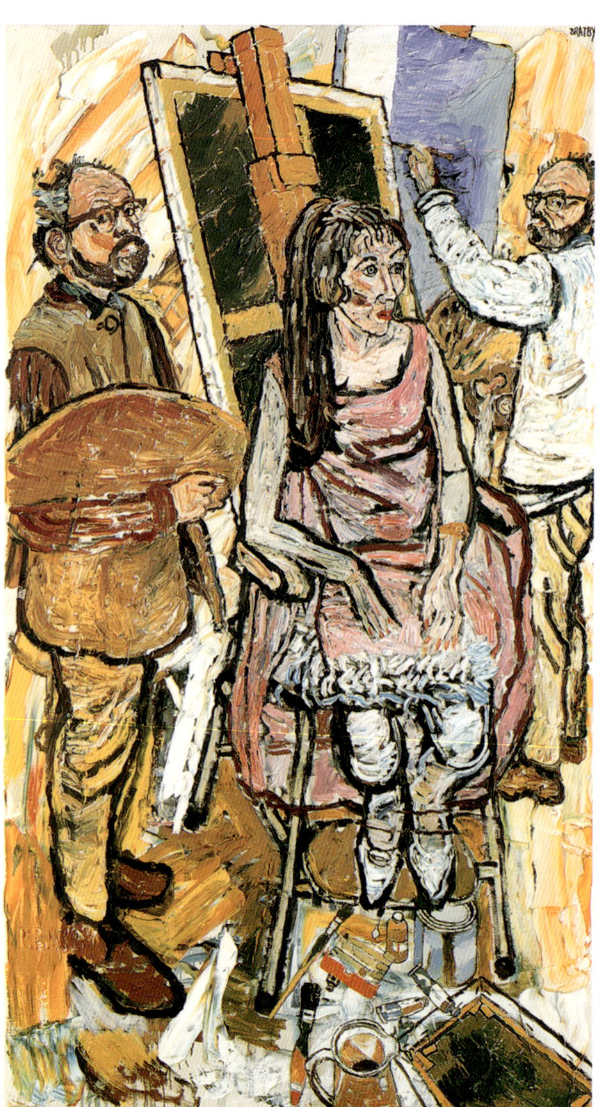

Vanitas: self-promotion and mortality

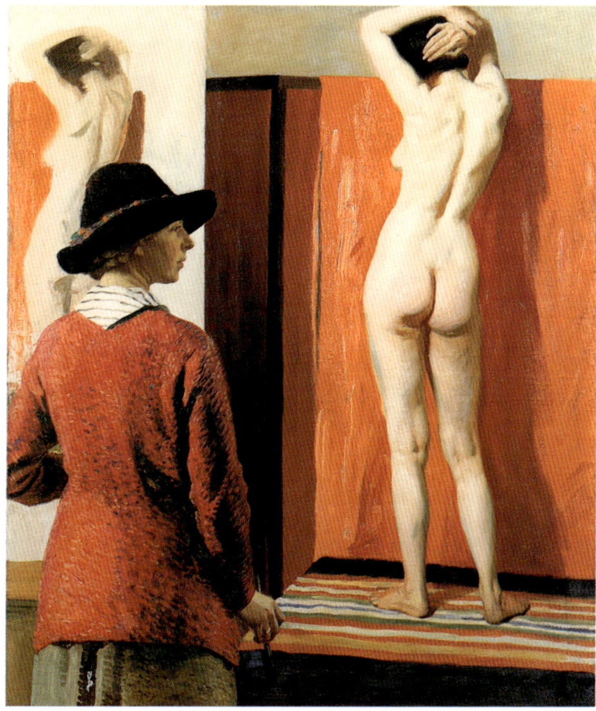

Dame Laura Knight
(1877–1970), 1913

This iconic work reasserts the importance of the model and promotes Knight's identity as a woman artist. She appears almost defiant in her now famous red cardigan (two-and-sixpence from a Penzance jumble sale). The complex composition showcases her skills, verticals and horizontals vibrating in tune to the colour attack of orange and red. A black hat defines her profile against the white of the unpainted canvas she is working on. The painting is big, deliberately designed to take up space, dominate and attract the viewer. This is in marked contrast to the self-portrait of her husband, Harold, which was painted ten years later (page 40).

Self-portraits

Thomas Kerrich
(1748–1828), 1774

A cleric and antiquary, Kerrich gained a scholarship to Italy where he made this work. Unlike Bratby's self-portrait, this image appears timeless. The unusual pose produces a powerfully theatrical and rather 'modern' effect. Transfixing the viewer with his gaze, Kerrich holds us in the present tense, seeming to defy death.

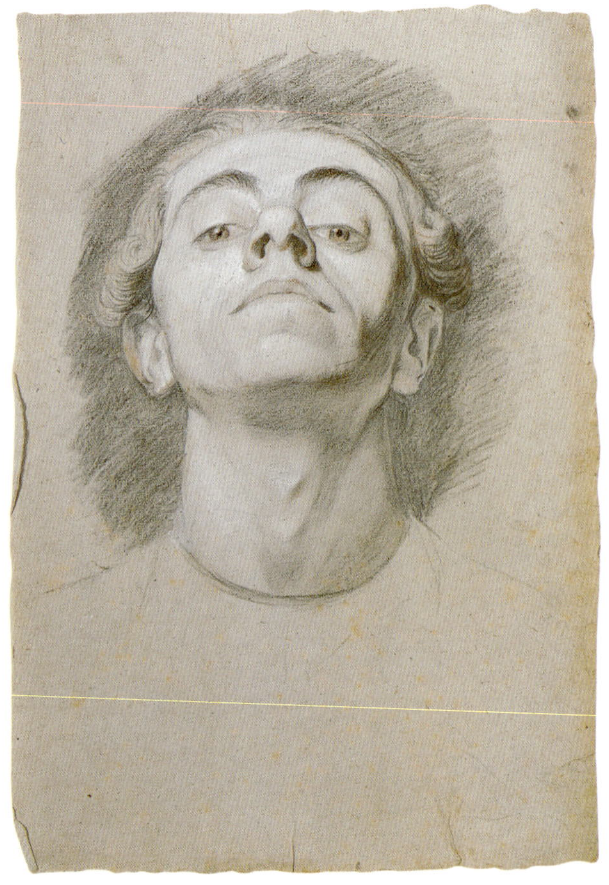

Opposite:
Julian Otto Trevelyan
(1910–88), 1940

A painter and printmaker, Trevelyan worked in Blackpool and Bolton on Tom Harrison's 'Mass Observation' project from 1937 to 1938. The choking smoke of the 'Satanic Mills' in this self-portrait ironically signifies his inspiration, but also the plight of those dwelling in the polluted atmosphere of the industrial North. In his autobiography *Indigo Days*, Trevelyan compares art to being a collaboration with the god of chance: 'if I am lucky, the picture will begin to paint itself'.

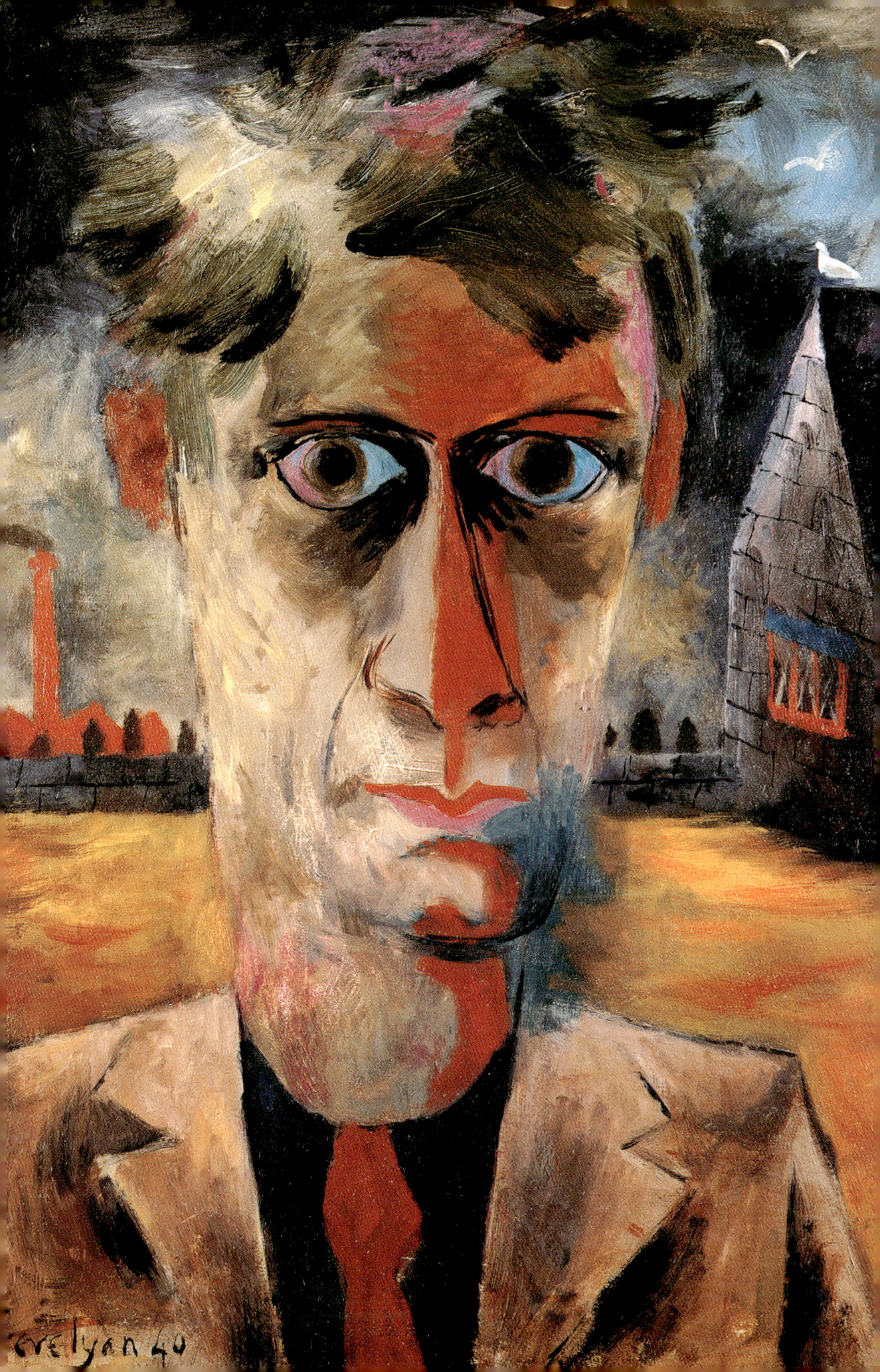

evelyn 40

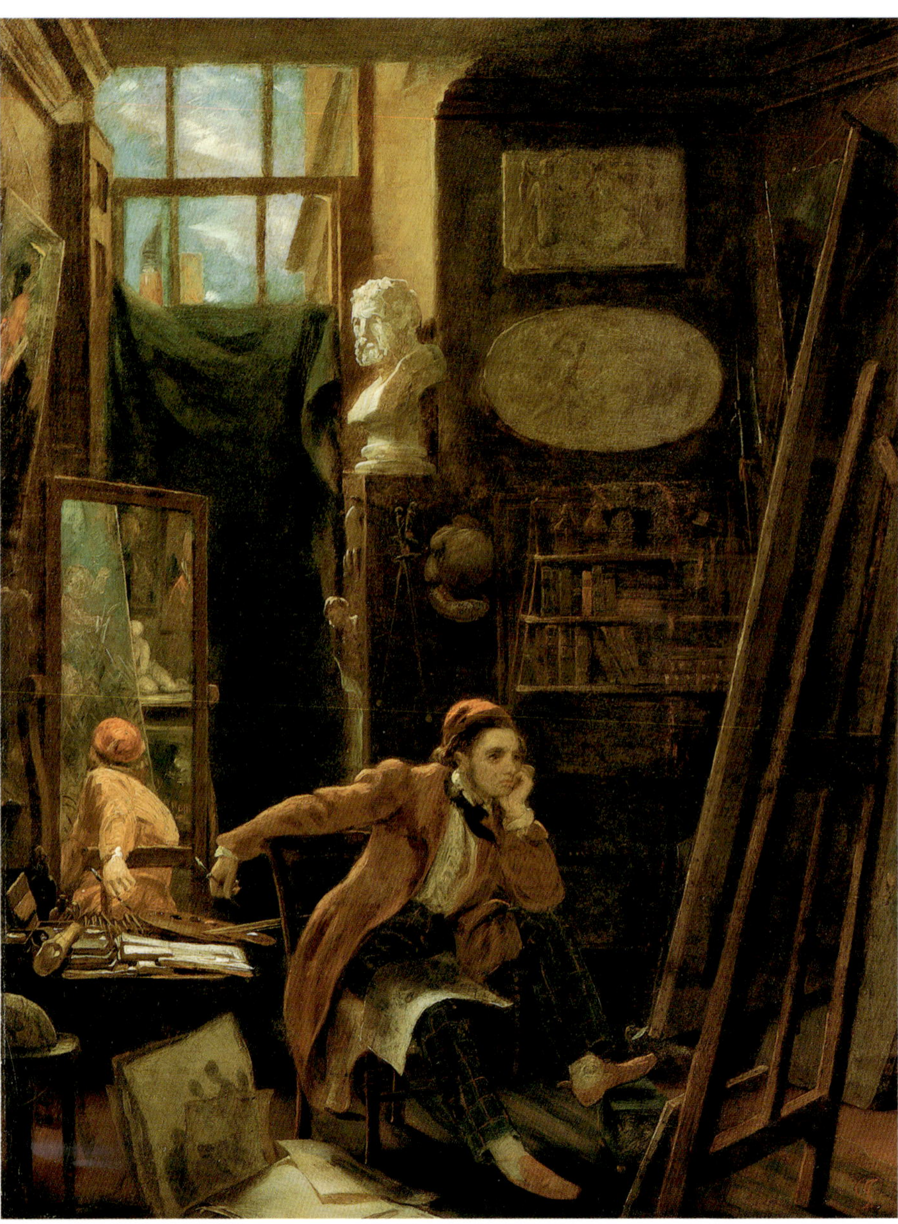

Chapter two
Mirrors and reflections

People – and artists in particular – have been fascinated by their own reflections since the earliest times. According to scientists, only humans and the chimpanzee can recognise their mirror image. Yet the manufacture of large non-distorting flat glass mirrors only began in the early sixteenth-century, in Venice. Prior to this, the Italian Renaissance architect and theorist Leon Battista Alberti (1404–72) commented on the use of water as reflector and receptor of the artist's gaze, stating that it was Narcissus who had been the real inventor of painting when he saw and fell in love with his reflection in the water. Narcissism is explored in psychoanalytical theory, and the self-portrait is its palpable extension. In 1916 Claude Monet (1840–1926) actually took a photograph capturing his own shadow on the surface of a pond. That same year he began painting his famous water lilies, the culmination of his life's work, a final manifestation of his being. A year later, at the age of seventy-seven, he went on to paint his last self-portrait.

In the rather claustrophobic self-portrait by James Sant reproduced here the mirror is positioned diagonally in the painting but directly behind the artist. The subject's centrally placed red cap, with its reflected image and the day-lit marble bust, create one of several triangular motifs within the composition. The inclusion of studio paraphernalia also recalls the much earlier work of Edward Collier (page 15) and Francis Hayman (page 47). The painted mirror offers a private view of a small nude modello; but the overriding mood of this self-portrait is one of self-absorption as the artist contemplates the work we see partially reflected behind him.

Mirrors are a critical element in the language of self-portraiture, as the works illustrated here show, whether recorded in the painting or merely implied. Gerlach Flicke acknowledges this in a Latin inscription above his self-portrait of 1554 'This he himself painted from a looking glass for his dear friends' (see page 46). The inclusion of a mirror in a picture naturally affects the visual composition, and can change the degree to which it reflects an alter-ego (the hidden, unconscious self) or is permitted to dominate and become the pivotal feature of the image.

In 1524 Parmigianino (1503–40) painted his *Self-Portrait in a Convex Mirror* (Kunsthistorisches Museum, Vienna) using a mirror that distorted his image and permitted him to show off his skills as a master of complex composition. Sir William Orpen echoes this work in his compact, delicate watercolour self-portrait of 1910. Mirrors and self-portraiture are recurring themes in Orpen's œuvre: in *The Mirror* (1900, Tate, London) he paints his then fiancée, Slade model Emily Scobel, seated below a convex mirror, rather like Whistler's portrait of his mother (1871; Musée d'Orsay, Paris). In his portrait of the Nicholsons, *A Bloomsbury Family* (1908; Scottish National Gallery of Modern Art), Orpen features his own reflection in a mirror, recalling Van Eyck's painting of the Arnolfinis.

The mirror is open to our gaze, but always beyond our reach. We sometimes forget that our view of ourselves is smaller and reversed in the mirror, and that we do not of course see ourselves as others do; furthermore, caught between mirrors, we can 'see' infinity stretching outwards. Exploring both the distortion and the infinite repetition, Italian artist Michelangelo Pistoletto (b.1933) used metallic paint as ground for his self-portraits in the early 1960s and then replaced it with polished steel. The mirror thus became a sculptural medium, integrating the viewer with the work in an exploration of the subjective nature of human perception and the relationship

Mirrors and reflections

Sir William Orpen
(1878–1931), 1910

Orpen was an original, technically brilliant and successful artist from Ireland. In this self-portrait, the green suggests a bilious fragility and transparency. Between Orpen's jawbone and his collar can be seen the hole left by the compass used to draw the circle. The work features a number of circles to connect the circular mirror conceit: this visual pun is reiterated as the artist reveals that he is working on the same picture that we are looking at – which in turn is the image he sees of himself in the mirror.

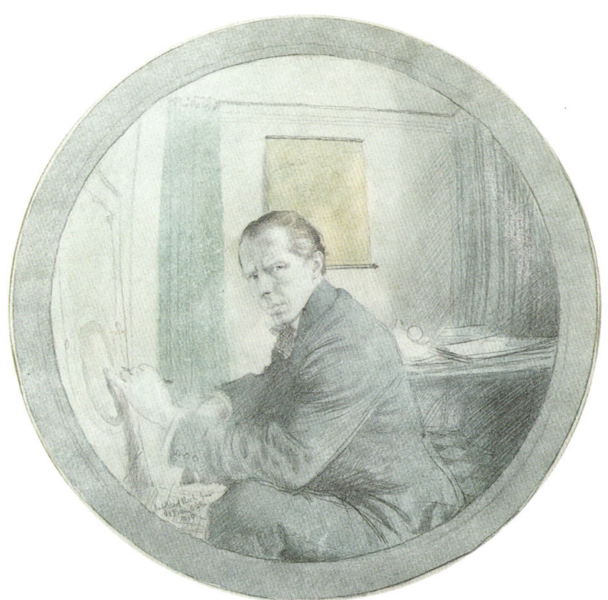

between reality and representation.

One might imagine that Bill Brandt employed a distorting mirror to create his bizarre photographs of nudes: in fact, he created these effects using a small-aperture wide-angle Kodak camera, originally used to photograph crime scenes. This equipment warps and distorts, producing abstractions that would not be out of place in a fairground. In his self-portrait of 1966 (page 28), Brandt continues to play with our perceptions by taking a mirror into the open air, simultaneously referring to the nude studies he collected together for the publication of his *Perspective of Nudes* in 1961.

Self-portraits

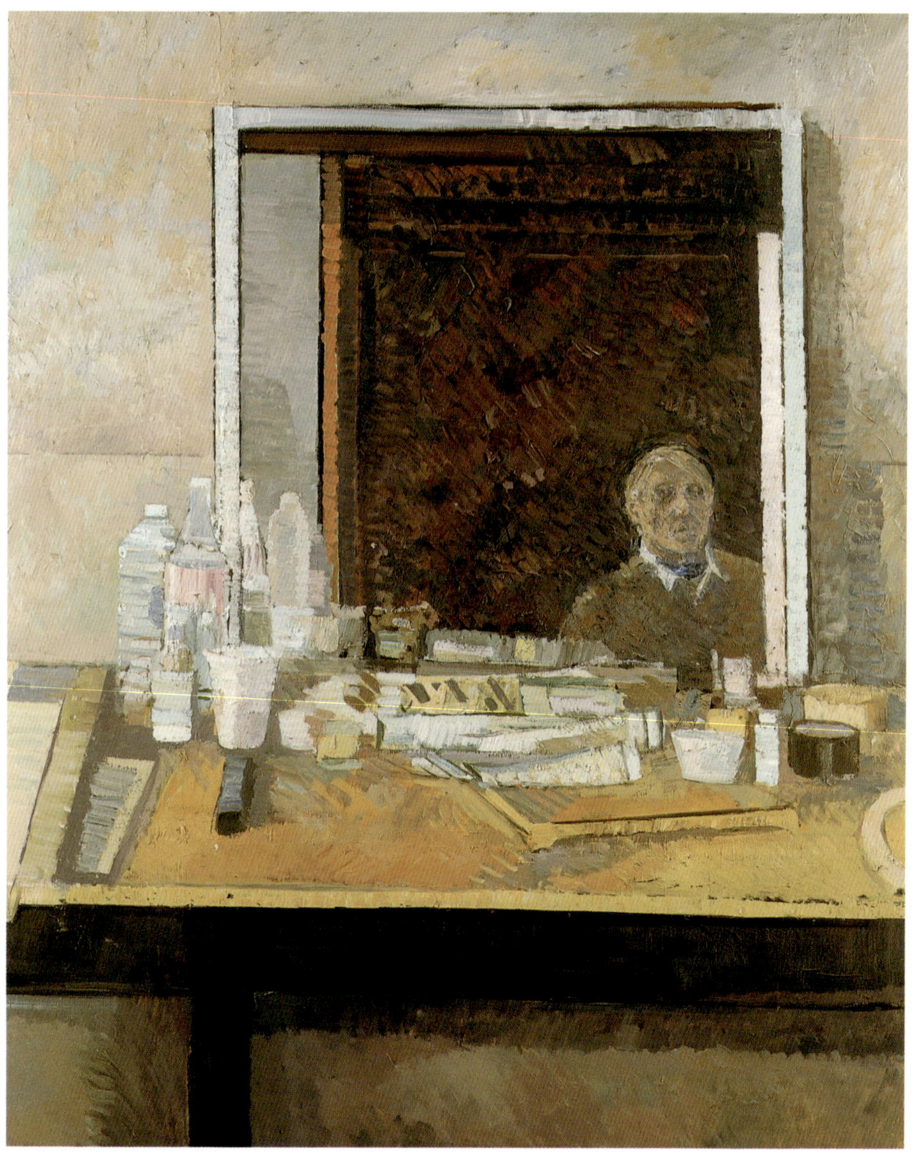

Mirrors and reflections

Opposite:
Sir Roger de Grey
(1918–95), 1990

Sir Roger de Grey was born into an aristocratic family and his uncle was the painter Spencer Gore (1878–1914). De Grey attended Eton and Chelsea School of Art, and was President of the Royal Academy of Arts between 1984 and 1993. This self-portrait, showing the influence of Cézanne, is characteristic of his work and is essentially a still-life reflected in a mirror. The low-key colours seem in keeping with the self-effacing self-image, and the greys might literally be taken as a reflection of the artist's name.

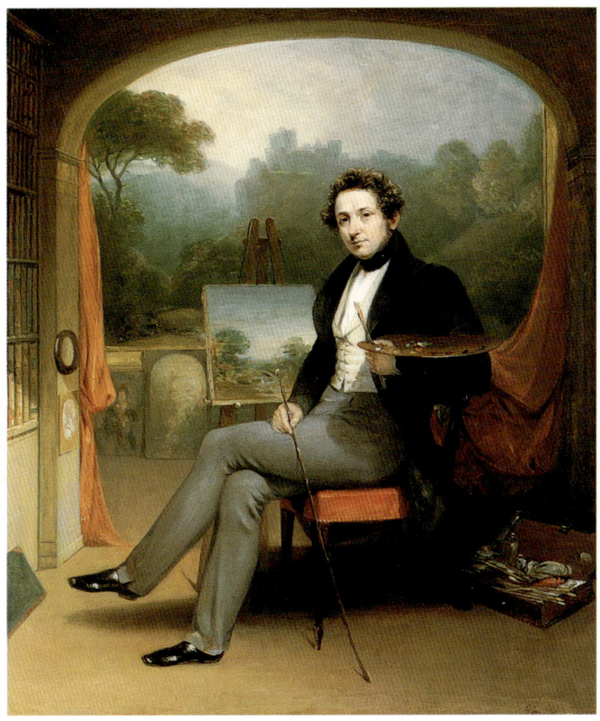

George Arnald
(1763–1841), 1831

Reflections play a complex role in this self-portrait. The viewer's eyes are drawn from Arnald's painting on the easel to the view of a romantic landscape, apparently seen out of the window; but the view is actually his own painting *Castle of Gloom* of 1814, inspired by Nicolas Poussin (1594–1665). Arnald is at work on a smaller version, further confusing our perceptions with this double *trompe l'oeil*. The unseen mirror suggests a false reality, and the artist manipulates our response to his 'reality'.

Bill Brandt
(1904–83), 1966

Taken on the East Sussex coast, this gritty black-and-white photograph seems deceptively simple, but is a complex and considered work. The shape of the chalk cliffs reflected in the mirror echoes that of the sitter's profile and contrasts with the textured shoreline and flat horizon, his head in chiaroscuro against the sky.

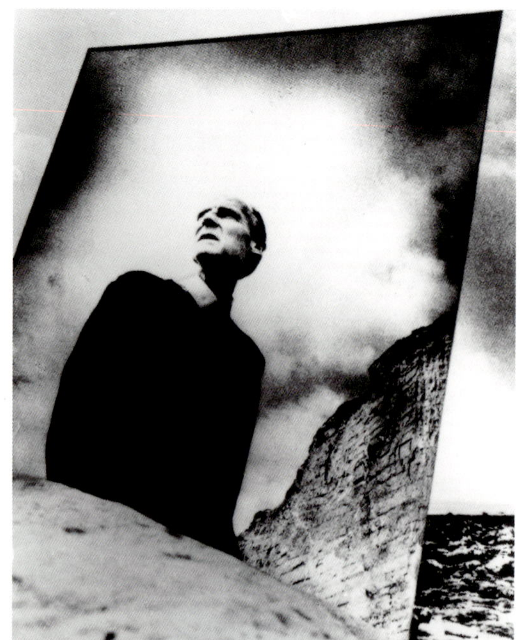

Harry Borden
(b.1965), 1998

The expanse of luscious green grass creates a sense of infinite space interrupted by stark tree shadows making calligraphic patterns among the autumn leaves. Borden almost cradles the large, heavy camera in an elegant, poetic gesture. A lone leaf is reflected at the top of the rectangular mirror. Like Brandt, his self-portrait illustrates a disorientating approach to what might be considered a very private engagement: both photographers have chosen an 'open' rather than a 'closed' outside space, whose definitions emanate from the boundaries of the mirror.

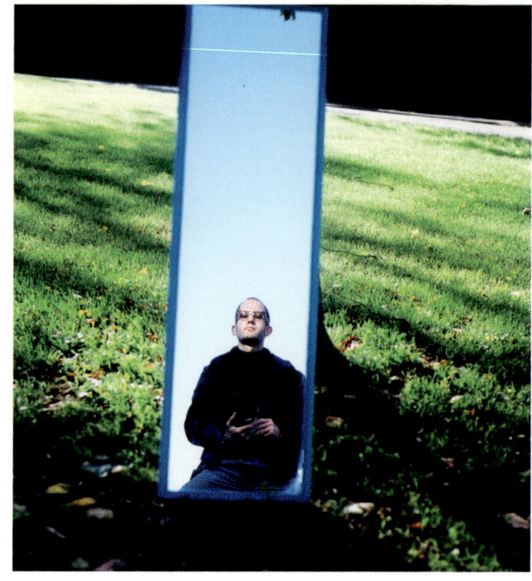

Mirrors and reflections

Malice through the looking glass
Mike McCartney
(b.1944) with Roberta (Bobby) Brown, 1962

This photograph was taken by Paul McCartney's brother Mike and includes Bobby Brown, who launched the Beatles' first official fan club. The form of the mirror is stronger than both figures: its shaped wings are dominant, enclosing the couple in an angelic embrace. The linear window pattern reflections contrast with the domestic regularity of the wallpaper, enhancing the feeling of enclosure.

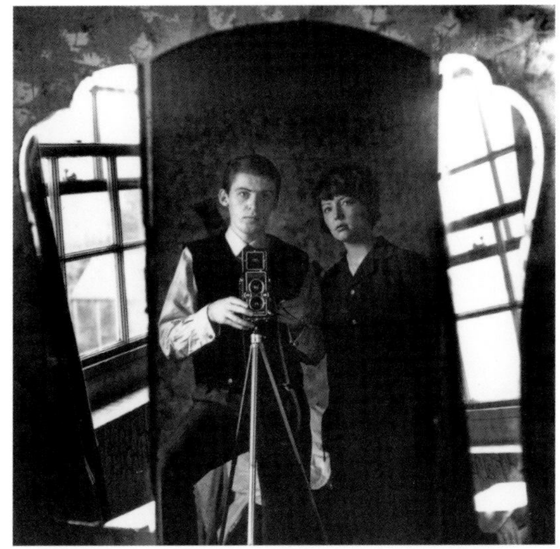

Pamela Chandler
(1928–93) with Mary Morris, 1963

As a staff photographer at the BBC, Chandler took this photograph in the make-up rooms at the Television Centre during rehearsals for *Anthony and Cleopatra*, with Morris as Cleopatra. By including herself reflected in the mirror, Chandler shares the intimacy of the pre-performance ritual of stepping into character. She said, 'It's amazing what a wonderful profession portrait photography is. You can become really close friends with clients; it is a very intimate thing.'

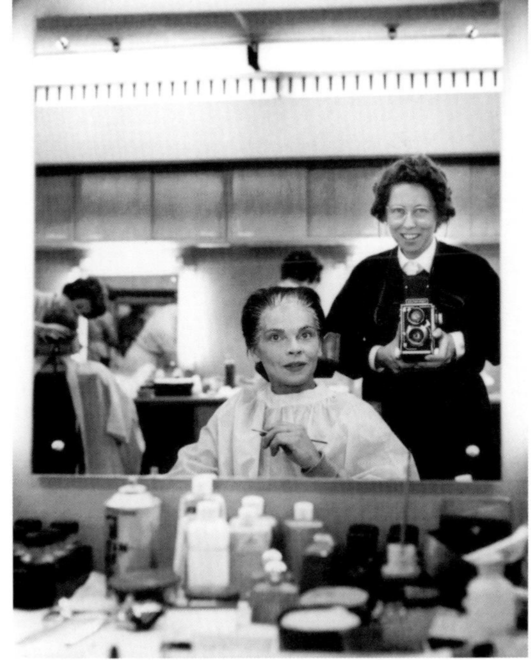

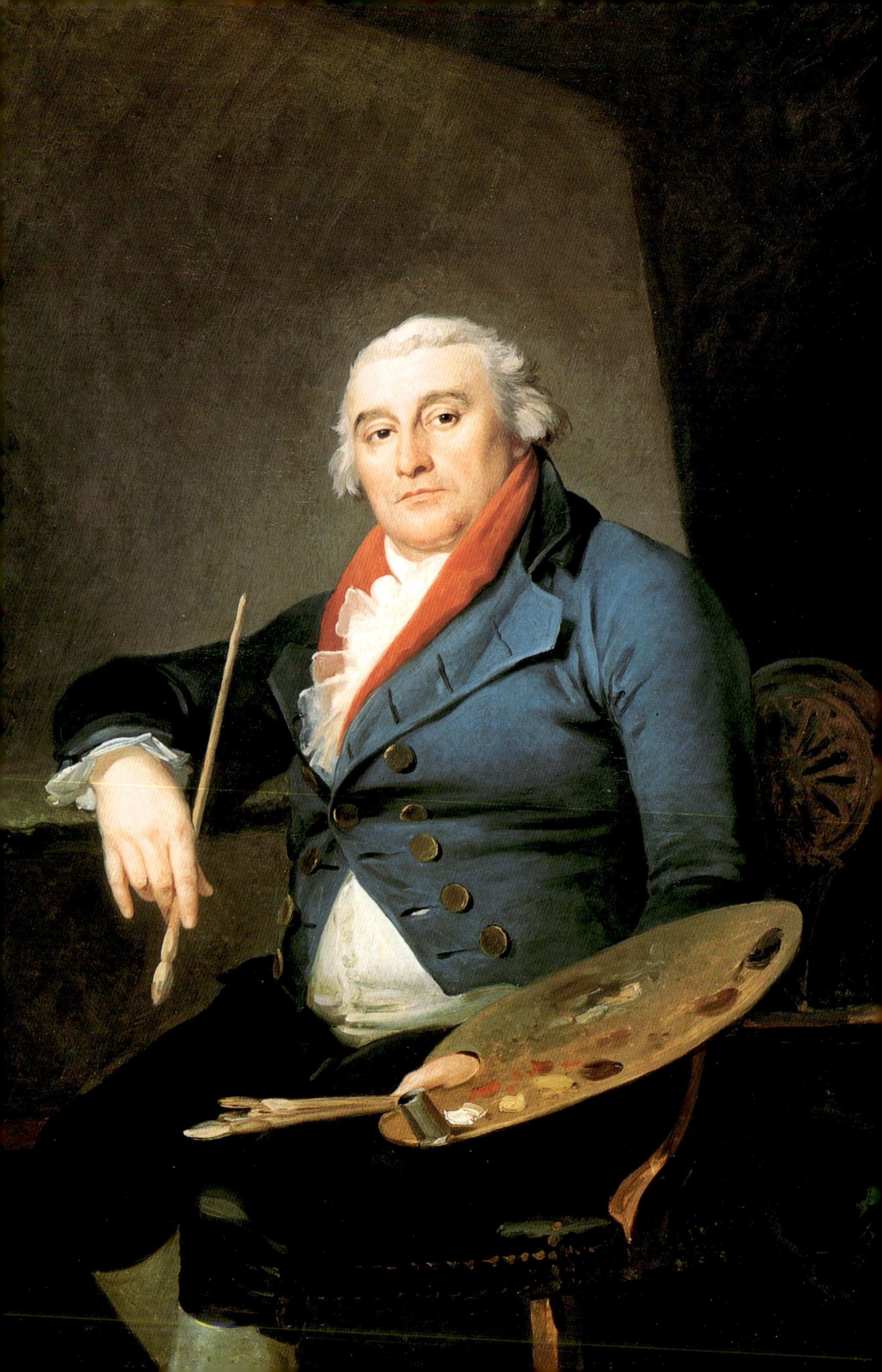

Chapter three
Dress and disguise

The choice of clothing in portraiture – particularly self-portraiture – is crucial. Should one dress up or down, in working clothes or Sunday best, or even fancy dress?

Changes in fashion are often reflected in portraiture, and have subsequently inspired dress codes in art. From the medieval sculptural effigies in chain mail and robes to Cindy Sherman's groundbreaking self-portraits of the 1980s, fashion, dressing up and disguise are part and parcel of the genre. Michelangelo Merisi da Caravaggio (1571–1610), for example, painted himself as Narcissus (1598–9; Galleria Nazionale d'Arte Antica, Rome), Henry Fuseli (1741–1825) sketched himself as a sculpted faun (1770s; Tate, London), and Sir Joshua Reynolds painted himself in his robes as a doctor of civil law (*c.*1780; Royal Academy of Arts).

In art as in life, clothing communicates: the portrayal of elegant fashions and sumptuous cloth in artists' self-portraits soon became an established formula to suggest wealth and status, and to attract the 'right' sort of client. Nicholas Hilliard (1547–1619) is elegant in his self-portrait of 1577 (Victoria and Albert Museum), recommending: 'let yr aparell be silke'. Unfortunately, despite the silk and superior clientele, when Hilliard was buried in St Martin-in-the-Fields in London in 1619 he had no fixed income, and very little to leave in his will.

Samuel Pepys (1633–1703) records buying an 'Indian gown' for his portrait sittings – his contemporary, Edward Collier favoured similar apparel (see page 15) – while Pepys's wife Elizabeth was portrayed 'like St Catherine'.

Costume can also be used to suggest status by association: Richard Cosway (1742–1821), who was a

Philippe Jacques de Loutherbourg
(1740–1812), *c.*1805–10

Born in Strasbourg, De Loutherbourg trained in Paris. He was a protégé of Denis Diderot (1713–84) and a member of the Académie Royale. Here he portrays himself as fashionably dressed in knee-length breeches – long trousers (pantaloons) were not acceptable court wear before 1815. His confident and distinguished demeanour compels the viewer to appreciate his talent. Having arrived in England from France in 1771, De Loutherbourg's palette is both patriotic and symbolic – Napoleon had standardised the colour of the French flag in 1804.

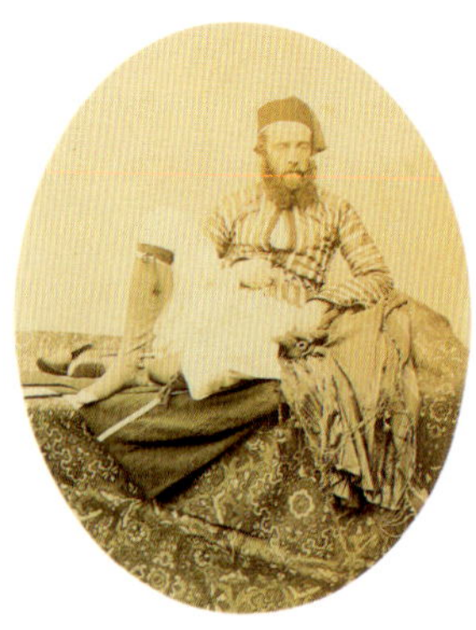

Francis Frith
(1822–98), 1857

Frith travelled to the East with his special portable darkroom, sometimes developing pictures in the cool of the tombs he photographed. In Akabar, he wore Arab garb sixty years before T.E. Lawrence. The image reproduced here appeared as the frontispiece to his two-volume publication *Egypt and Palestine photographed and described by Francis Frith* (London, 1858–9). He fulfilled Baudelaire's idea that photography should 'enrich the tourist's album and restore to his eye the precision which his memory may lack'.

member of the 'Macaroni' set, famous for their fashionable excesses, depicted himself dressed in Van Dyck mode (*c.*1770; National Trust, Attingham Park, Shropshire) – thus paying public homage to the great painter while suggesting artistic status for himself by association. Sir Anthony van Dyck (1599–1641) was famous for his sartorial display: he was described by contemporary writer Giovanni Pietro Bellori as wearing 'fine stuffs', adorning his head with feathers and imitating the splendour of Zeuxis.

Cosway's contemporary Philippe Jacques de Loutherbourg came to London in 1771 and worked for the actor-manager David Garrick producing special effects, culminating in his invention in 1782 of the Eidophusikon. This magical miniature theatre was a precursor of the diorama and a kind of eighteenth-century equivalent to film. His theatrical background, however, is not reflected in the formal clothing that he wears in his self-portrait.

Photographer Francis Frith is pictured languidly reclining on cushions in the manner of an oriental painting. This extraordinary man made his fortune in groceries and then became a photographer. As a Quaker he was concerned to make his location photographs as truthful as possible, often incorporating people for scale.

Richard Cockle Lucas's primary medium was sculpture. He also made etchings, designed his own house, and wrote and created an entire album of carte-de-visite 'fancy-dress' self-portraits much in the manner of Wilkie Wynfield (page 94).

Cecil Beaton was an enthusiastic self-portraitist, passionate about extravagant decor and complex detail, from masks and mirrors to fabrics and decorated backgrounds (see page 36). He depicted himself variously as a scarecrow, an old lady (as a distorted reflection in the funnel of a Mediterranean yacht) and in Vanitas mode wearing a ruff and

Dress and disguise

Brian Griffin
(b.1948), 1988

The fur fringe around the artist's hood bears a resemblance to eyelashes, suggesting the eye of the camera. Griffin's clever manipulation of the viewer's reading of his portrait is innovative. 'I remember wanting to depict myself at the time as a spikey sea urchin. I guess it was taken ... when I didn't want anyone to get near me, both psychologically or physically.'

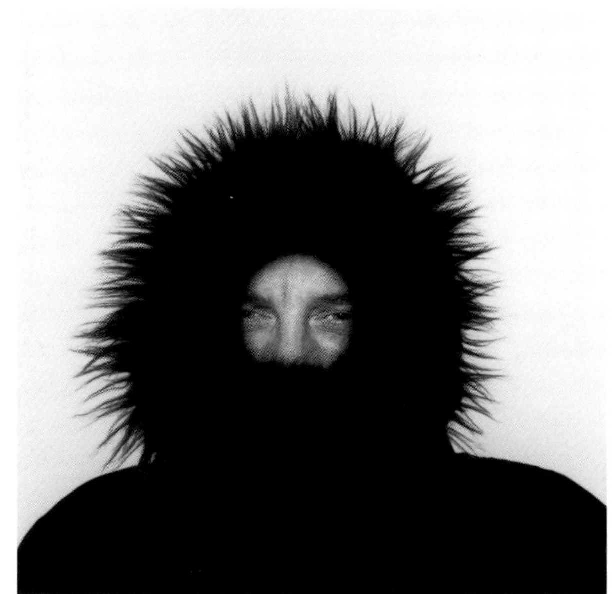

holding a globe and a skull.

Doris Zinkeisen and her younger sister Anna (known as 'Big' and 'Little Zinc') worked on a number of projects together, including painting murals for the *Queen Mary*. Beautiful and talented self-publicists, the Zinkeisens were both photographed by the fashionable Dorothy Wilding and Madame Yevonde (see pages 72–3 and 74–5). In Doris's self-portrait (page 41) she depicts herself wearing a colourful Chinese embroidered shawl. Fashion items such as this were imported for the European market and were popular during the 1930s, but are also a visual gift to a decorative artist.

In her 2001 self-portrait, Sam Taylor-Wood (page 37) by contrast wears the classic gentleman's lounge suit giving her the air of a sharply dressed businesswoman and emphasising the incongruous nature of her prop, the stuffed hare.

Self-portraits

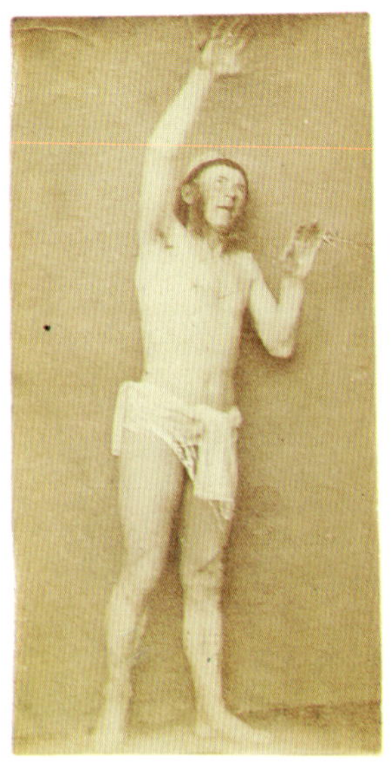

As a Martyr to the Truth
Richard Cockle Lucas
(1800–83), *c*.1858

Cockle Lucas's portraits use clothing as a device, not as confirmation of actual journeys, like Frith, but for fantastical imaginary situations, employing different facial expressions and guises. This photograph shows him in a loincloth, arms stretched heavenwards. Originally apprenticed to learn the trade of carving knife handles, he became a prolific sculptor, specialising in both medallions and portrait busts.

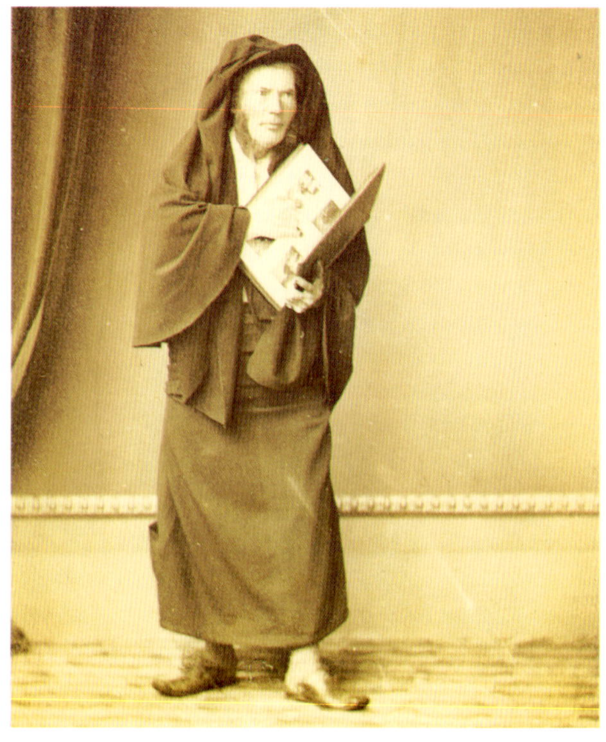

As a Devotee of Art
Richard Cockle Lucas
(1800–83), *c*.1858

Here Cockle Lucas is swathed in monk-like robes, clasping an illustrated album in one hand and pointing to the pictures with the other. This could be a version of the green leather-bound album in the National Portrait Gallery's collection, which contains forty-two of his surreal and often bizarre self-portraits.

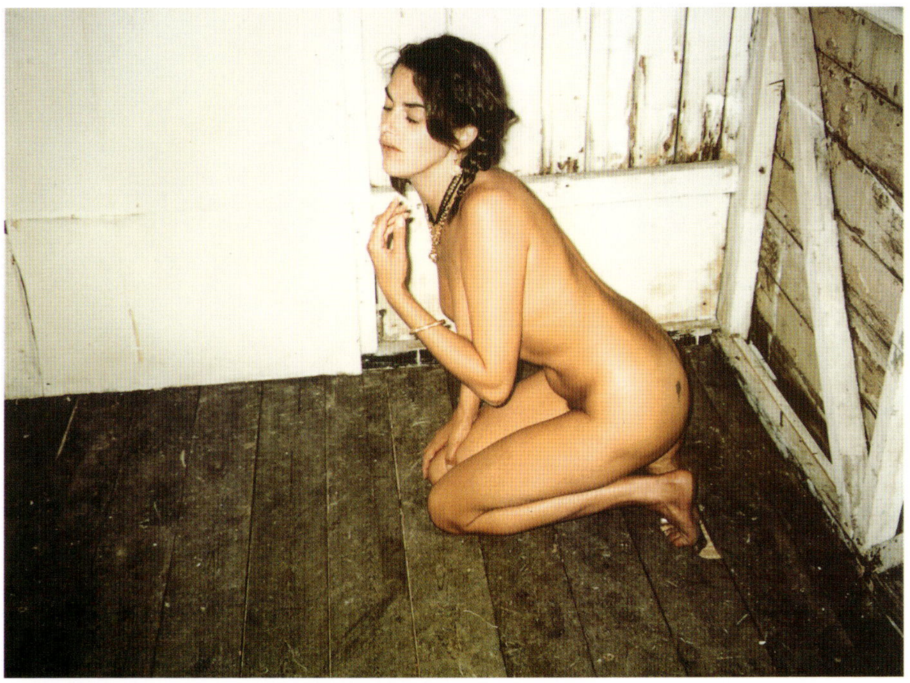

The Last Thing I said to you is don't leave me here. 1
Tracey Emin
(b.1963), 2000

Tracey Emin frequently uses herself as subject matter for her art. She
has a penchant for cryptic, misspelt pieces of text in her sewn works
and drawings, which bear her written signature. This self-portrait taken
in a beach hut hints at her Margate origins, the enclosed space
reinforcing the claustrophobic atmosphere that surrounds this very
public artist. Her nudity, both provocative and vulnerable, establishes
the ambiguity suggested by the title.

Self-portraits

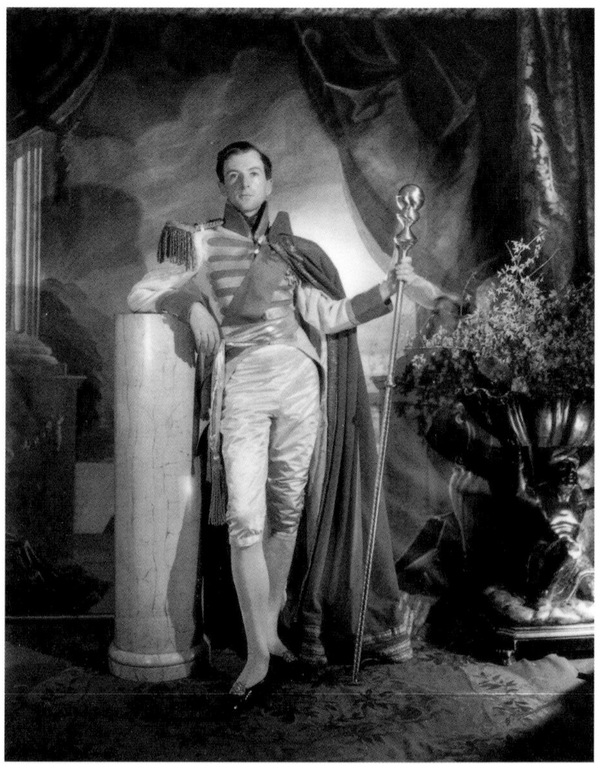

Cecil Beaton
(1904–80), 1933

In this photograph, taken at the Opera Ball at the Metropolitan Opera House, New York, Beaton exploits the theatrical fantasy of dressing up. At once related to a certain tradition of camp divas, pantomime dames and cross-dressing, Beaton is nevertheless fully aware of contemporary developments by the Surrealists and portraits *en travesti* by Marcel Duchamp and others.

Dress and disguise

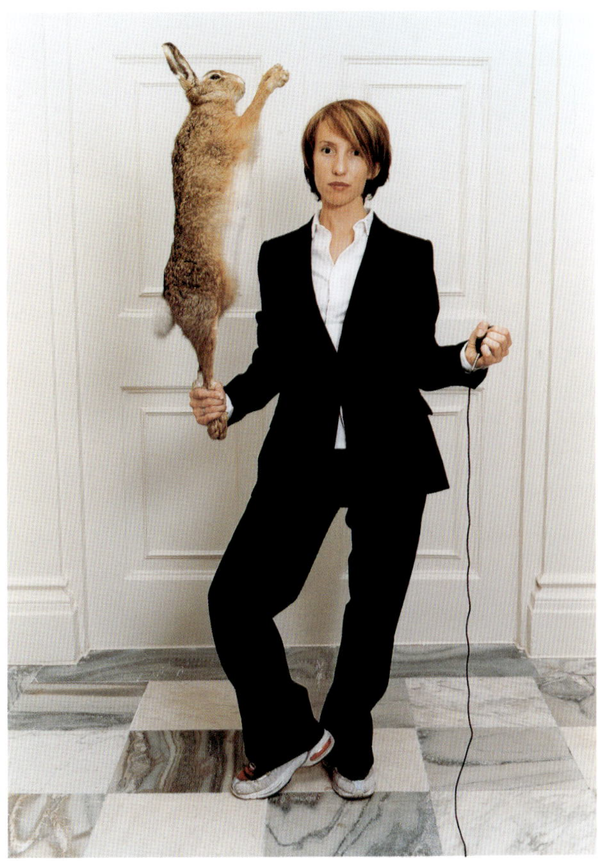

Self Portrait in a Single Breasted Suit with Hare
Sam Taylor-Wood
(b.1967), 2001

Sam Taylor-Wood is sometimes known for her links with the glitterati and the international party scene. Yet her art aspires to a more serious tone. This image was created following her treatment for breast cancer. In an interview, she described the symbolism in her choice of props and attire: 'With chemotherapy, the first thing you think is that you are going to lose your hair. The hare symbolises lust and passion, so here I am with a head of hair, in a single-breasted suit, holding on to lust and passion.'

Self-portraits

Wyndham Lewis
(1882–1957), 1932

A draughtsman, painter and
author, Lewis was a volatile and
charismatic artist whose
collaborative publication *Blast*
(1914) was the manifesto of his
Vorticist movement. This large
book, with vivid pink cover and
modern graphics, was designed
for maximum impact. Here
he intentionally dons a slightly
sinister looking expression
and hat for a self-portrait to
accompany a typically
provocative article for the *Daily
Herald* entitled, 'What it feels like
to be an Enemy'.

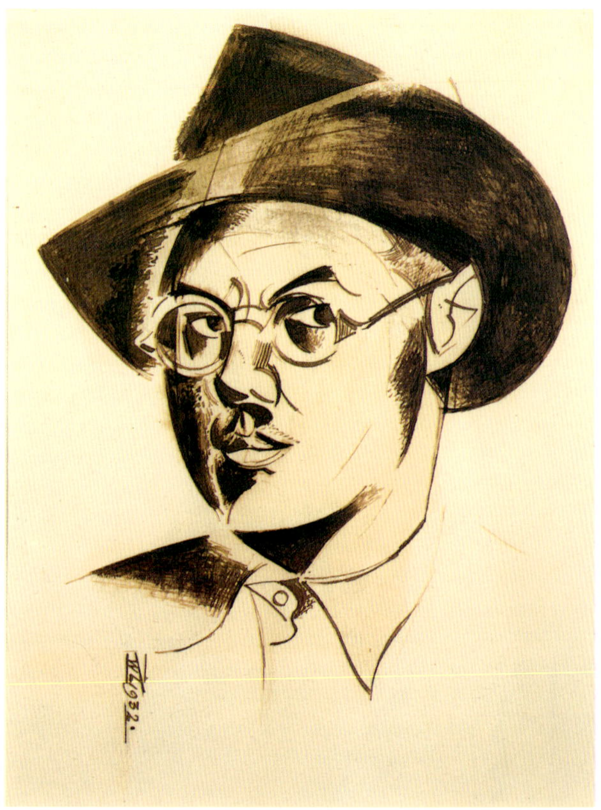

Opposite:
Lee Miller
(1907–77), 1943

A woman at ease both in front of the camera and behind it, Lee Miller
was well aware of the importance of the reproduced image: she
worked for British and American *Vogue*, both as a model and
a photographer, and between 1940 and 1945 she worked as a war
photographer and correspondent in France and Germany. Assisted
by her colleague and lover David E. Scherman (1916–97), this self-
portrait was taken in Portsmouth whilst they were working on the
book *Wrens in Camera* (1945). Miller captures herself in an intimate
moment as the off-duty working woman, pyjamas unbuttoned,
well-earned drink in hand. In April 1945 she and Scherman were
among the first to enter the concentration camp at Dauchau, taking
photographs that shocked the world.

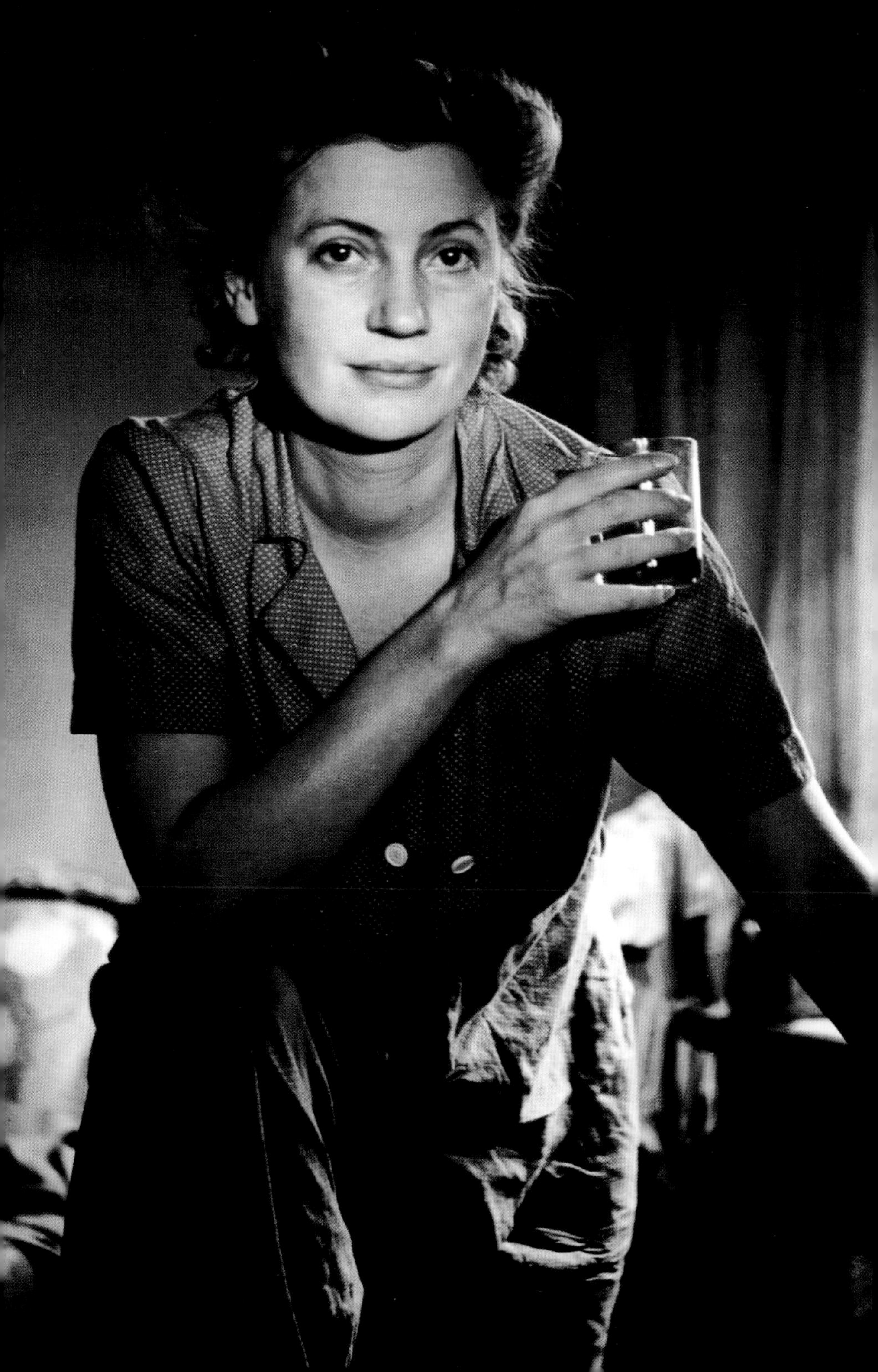

Harold Knight
(1874–1961), *c*.1923

An elegant, meticulous painter,
Harold Knight is depicted in a
dun-coloured overcoat, texturally
suited to his even, modulated
brushwork; only a touch of green
and red relieve the monotony.
A conscientious objector during
the First World War, Knight's
health suffered as a result of
working as a farm labourer. The
glint of his glasses here suggests
his intelligent dogmatism, ever
the foil to the perennial
exuberance of his wife, Dame
Laura Knight (see page 19). His
signature on the stretcher of
the canvas behind him in the
painting is possibly a light touch
in an otherwise serious work.

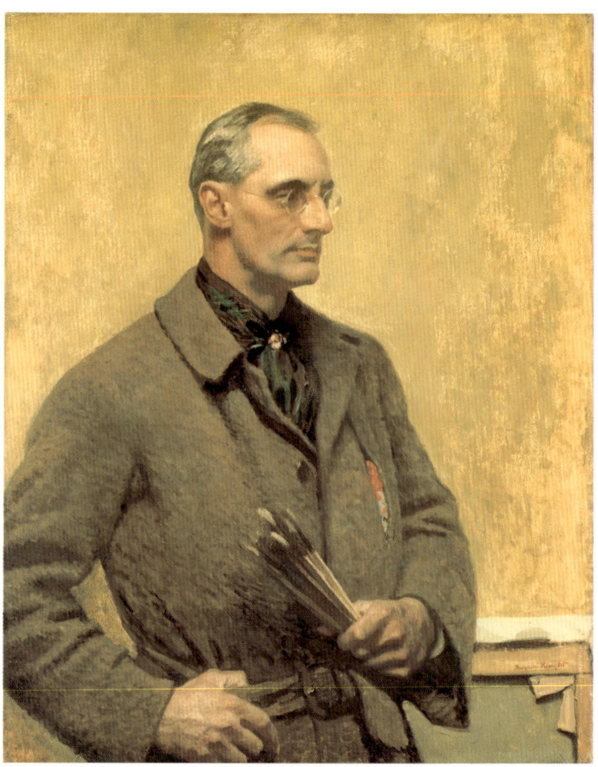

Opposite:
Doris Zinkeisen
(1898–1991), exhibited 1929

Doris Zinkeisen wears a Chinese embroidered shawl, which
dominates the painting and emphasises her revealing décolletage.
The dramatic double sweep of the white sheet contrasts with the
shawl's vibrant pattern, hinting at her theatrical work and reflecting a
knowledge of body language. The shawl's fringe draws attention to
her elegant hands tapering to red painted nails, which in turn are
echoed in her blood-red lipstick.

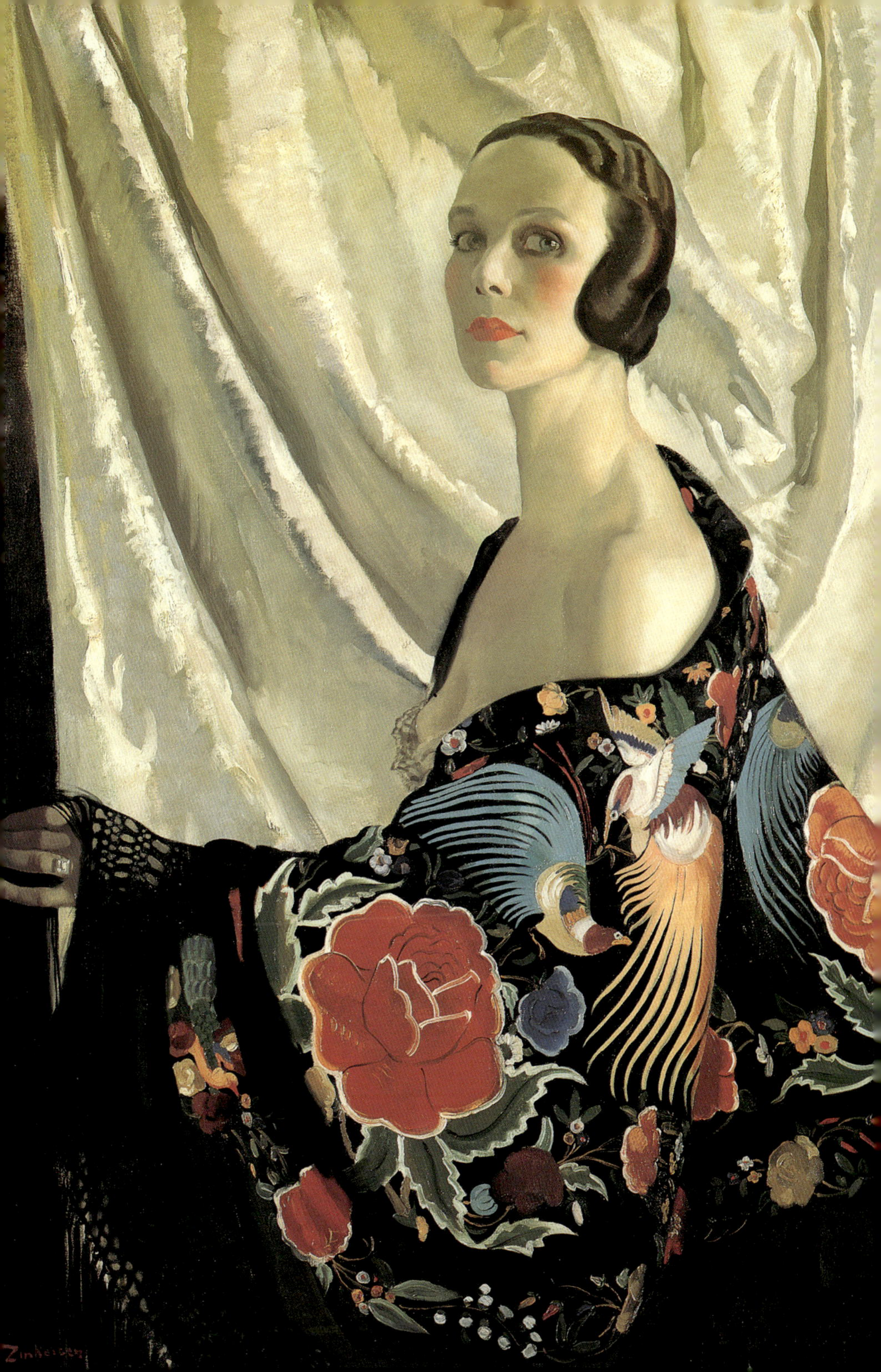

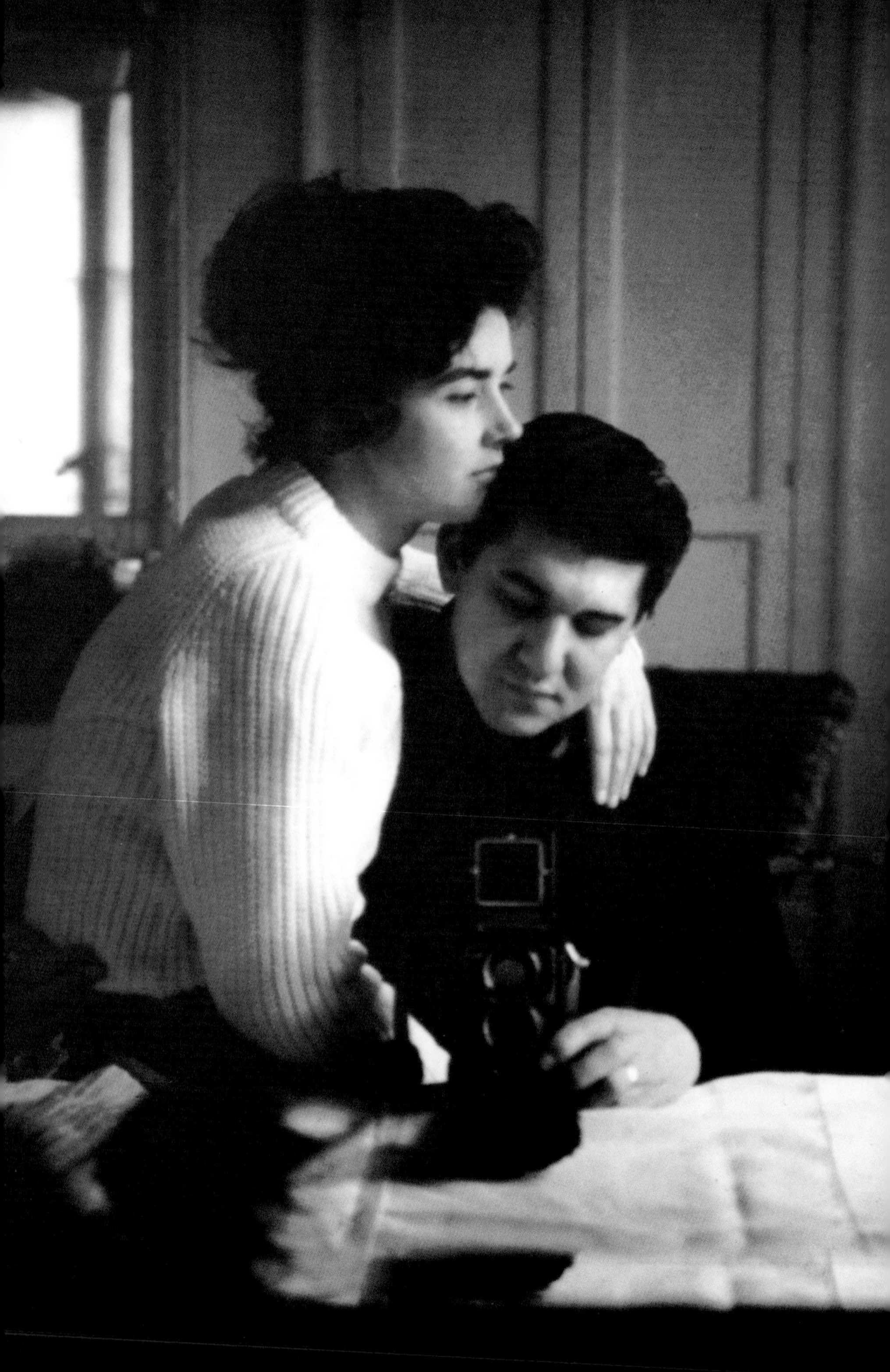

Chapter four
Friends and family

Why would an artist want to make a self-portrait that includes someone else? There could be any number of specific reasons, but the primary intention will surely be to record people and relationships in the artist's life at a specific moment in time. Velázquez's *Las Meninas* (1656) is perhaps the most famous self-portrait within this category: in it the hierarchy of the Spanish court is revealed. Isolated from the group are King Philip IV and Queen Mariana, with the artist at his easel, all portrayed within the context of the court. Velázquez wears the Cross of the Order of Santiago, a great honour that he received three years after the painting was completed. This later addition testifies to his promotion to nobility as well as his artistic genius.

The self-portrait can be compared to a diary: a personal and exclusive viewpoint rarely produced with publication in mind, within which relationships and emotions may be explained and analysed. Similarly, some self-portraits reveal artists' attitudes to social hierarchies and situations; double 'love' portraits evoke parity, paintings of the artist with his wife becoming current in Northern Europe in the fifteenth century. Lewis Morley's self-portrait is a tribute to love: his wife Pat sits on his knee, their intimacy reinforced by the glow of a piece of white paper, which acts as the pivotal light source linking the composition from the window to Pat's white jumper.

Double and group portraits often allude to an activity connecting the sitters. Francis Hayman depicts himself as being highly attentive towards his manifestly wealthy patron, the elegantly dressed and somewhat portly Grosvenor Bedford (see page 47). The artist focuses the viewer's attention on the protagonists by showing them engrossed in viewing and discussing a work on an easel that is angled away

Lewis Morley (b.1925)
with Patricia Morley (b.1931),
1959

Known for his iconic photograph of Christine Keeler seated naked on an Arne Jacobsen chair (1963), Morley proffers a different type of intimacy in this double portrait, taken at the Hotel Marechal Ney, Montparnasse, Paris. He depicts himself gazing into his Rolleiflex camera to see the hotel room reflected back at him through the unseen mirror. Recalling this occasion, Pat Morley commented that the distant expression on her face was one of exhaustion rather than dreamy romance – the couple had spent the whole day sightseeing.

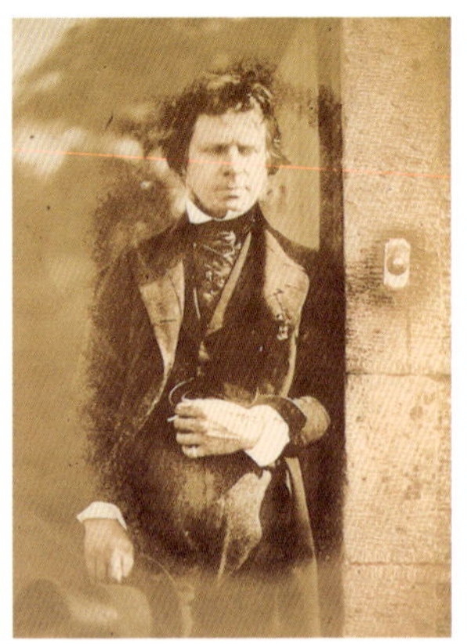

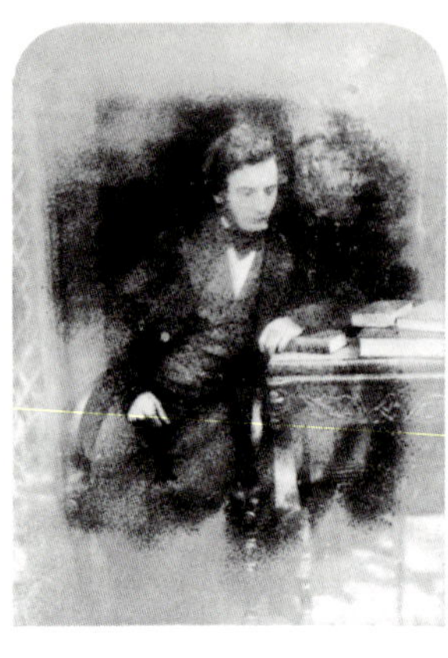

(above): **David Octavius Hill**
(1774–1852), *c.*1843
(below): **Robert Adamson**
(1821–48), 1843–8

Adamson trained initially as an
engineer. Sir David Brewster
introduced him to Hill and
remarked that Adamson's
'photographs have all the force
and beauty of the sketches of
Rembrandt'. In Hill & Adamson's
album, Adamson's self-portrait is
the frontispiece to Volume III,
and Hill's appears at the start of
Volumes I and II.

from us. Hayman's studio is full of fashionable items,
including a mahogany armchair for his visitor. On the
table behind them are two sculptures, a bust and what
could be a copy of the Uffizi Crouching Venus, a foil
for the rather risqué Rococo painting of Venus and
Mars hanging on the wall above. The composition
of this double portrait is based on *Le Portrait*, an
engraving after Claude Gillot (1673–1722): Hayman
is thus showing off his intellectual pretensions by
revealing his knowledge of French art.

Gerlach Flicke, by contrast, is in either the Tower
of London or Marshalsea prison (probably for debt)
and portrays himself with a palette alongside his
cellmate Henry Strangwish, who holds a lute
(page 46). Little is known of these two friends; the
implication is that they are equal partners in the arts
if not in crime. Certainly, the two figures occupy
equal space within the diptych and share the same
azurite blue backdrop.

If prison is at one end of the spectrum of shared
experience, that represented by Gawen Hamilton's
A Conversation of Virtuosis ... at the Kings Arms (1735;
page 48) is altogether at the other. The sitters in this
group portrait paid money to be included in this
gathering of like-minded artists. All wear wigs – de
rigueur for much of the eighteenth century – except
for Hamilton, who distinguishes himself from the
crowd by wearing a cap. Wigs were symbolic of
non-manual status: the cap denotes an artistic or
literary man.

Working relationships between artists are perhaps
rarer than in other professions. A number of
distinguished partnerships are nevertheless recorded
in self-portraits, such as those of the Smiths of
Chichester (page 52) or the multifarious imagery of
Gilbert and George. The Smith brothers George and
John often painted canvases together and here show
themselves hard at work on one of the landscapes that

In the Piss
Gilbert (b.1943) **& George**
(b.1942), 1997

Naked but for Gilbert's watch and George's glasses, the two men stand before an abstract backdrop derived from a microscopic sample of their urine; they are literally *In the Piss*, as the title of the work implies. They are also perhaps 'on the piss' – getting drunk as they did in a video made in 1972 entitled *Gordon's makes us Drunk* (Tate, London), where the artists are shown seated at a table, drinking gin to a soundtrack of Elgar and Grieg. Gilbert and George use accumulated images of themselves as their artistic signature and never allow themselves to be shown apart. Their photoworks are always meticulously signed, dated and titled.

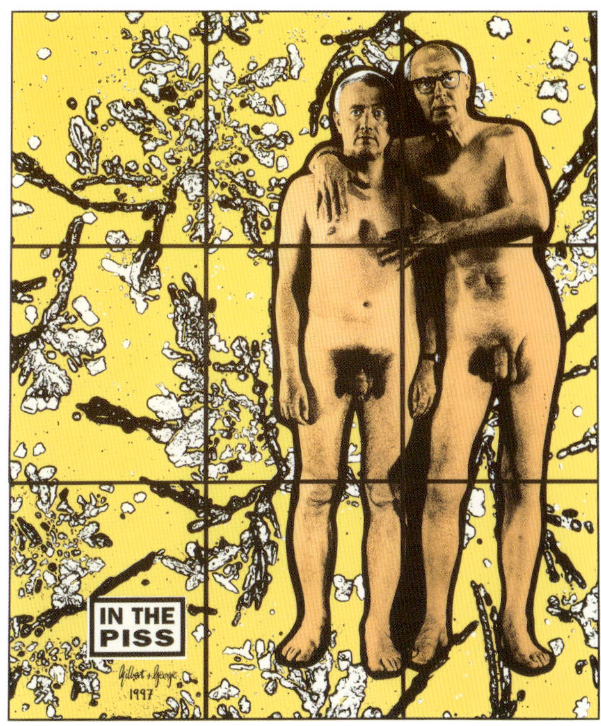

provided their subject matter. The partnership of David Octavius Hill and Robert Adamson flourished for five years, during which they took in excess of 3,000 photographs. The symbiotic nature of their working practice was defined in 1844 when they first showed their calotypes at the Royal Scottish Academy, these were credited as being 'executed by R. Adamson under the artistic direction of D.O. Hill'.

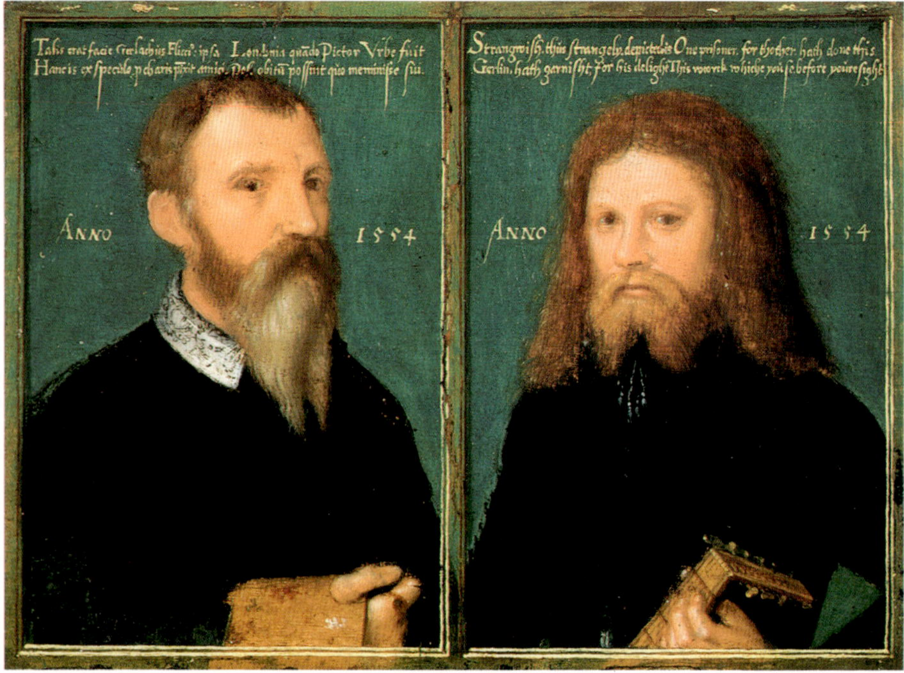

Gerlach Flicke
(*fl.*1545; d.1558) and Henry Strangwish (d.1562), 1554

The Latin inscription that Flicke painted above his head translates as:
'Such was the face of Gerlach Flicke when he was a painter in the City
of London. This he himself painted from a looking glass for his dear
friends. That they might have something by which to remember him
after his death'. Little is known about Flicke: he was German, from
Osnabrück, and came to work as a portrait painter in England.
Strangwish was a privateer from a distinguished West Country family.
After having survived a death sentence in 1559 (the execution was
stayed), he died from injuries sustained in the English attack on Rouen
in October 1562.

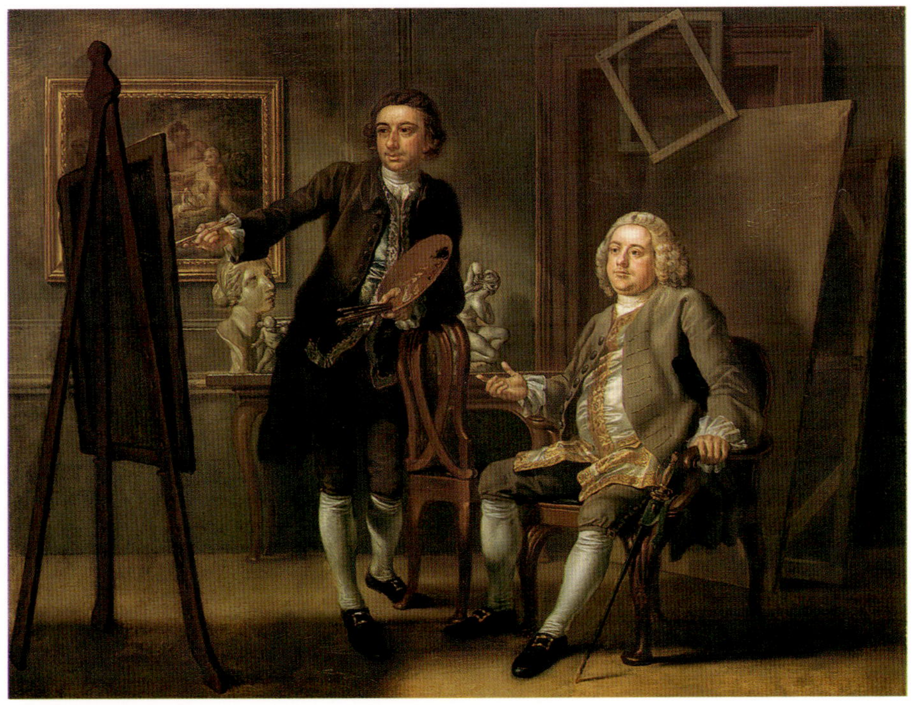

Francis Hayman
(1708–86) and Grosvenor Bedford (1708–71), *c*.1748–50

Hayman gives us an intimate view both of his studio and of his
business practice as he talks his patron Grosvenor Bedford through a
new painting on the easel. Although ostensibly a private scene, there
is a suspiciously self-conscious air about both the elegantly dressed
pair and the unnaturally neat surroundings of the artist's studio.
Hayman's relaxed conversation pieces were a considerable influence
on the early work of Thomas Gainsborough.

Self-portraits

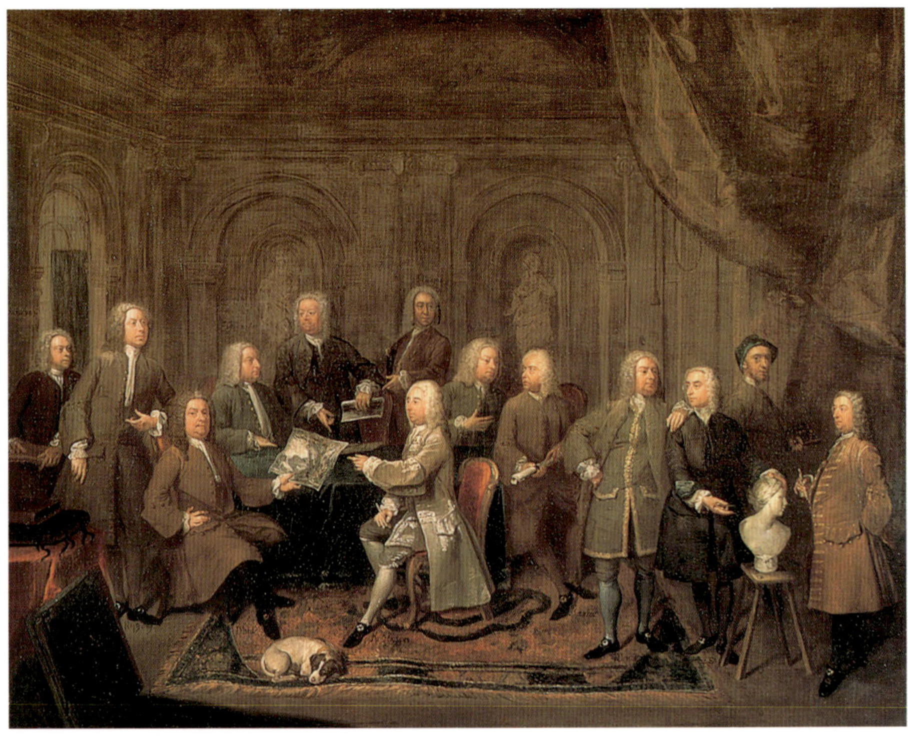

***A Conversation of Virtuosis ... at the Kings Arms
(A Club of Artists)*, Gawen Hamilton** (*c*.1697–1737), 1735

Hamilton (wearing a blue cap) specialised in conversation pieces and this is his best-known work in the genre. When completed, the painting was raffled to the artist subscribers. Michael Dahl is seated third from the left (note how he has aged by comparison with his self-portrait on page 64).

Opposite:
Margaret MacGregor 'Peggy' Angus (1904–93)
with James Ramsay MacDonald and members of his family, 1930s

Designer and painter Peggy Angus was a friend of the Labour Party's first Prime Minister, James Ramsay MacDonald. She portrays herself here standing and singing next to the piano in a family evening at home. The muted autumnal colours lend a cosy air: the red tablecloth, like the central red seat cover in Hamilton's painting, acts as focal point to the group. Both works show the artists functioning in their own contemporary milieu and the formulation of a sort of environmental self-portraiture.

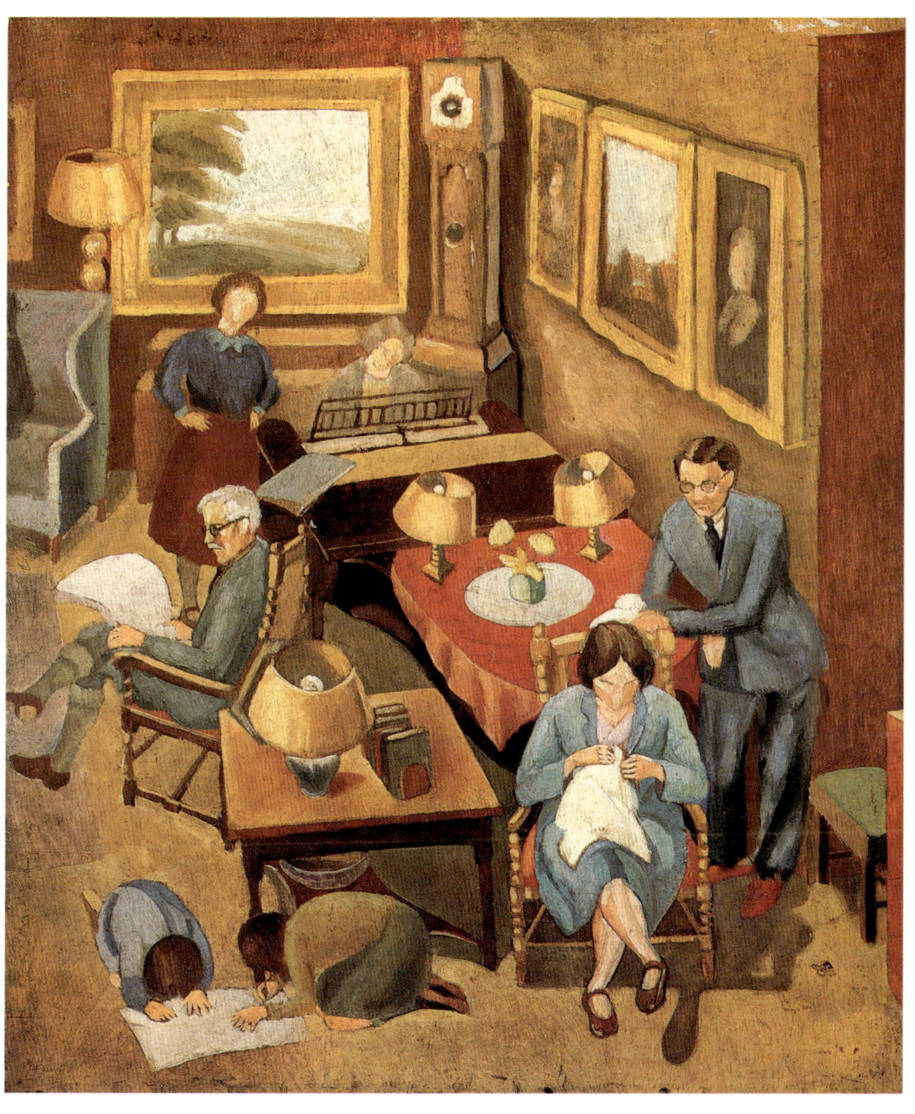

Self-portraits

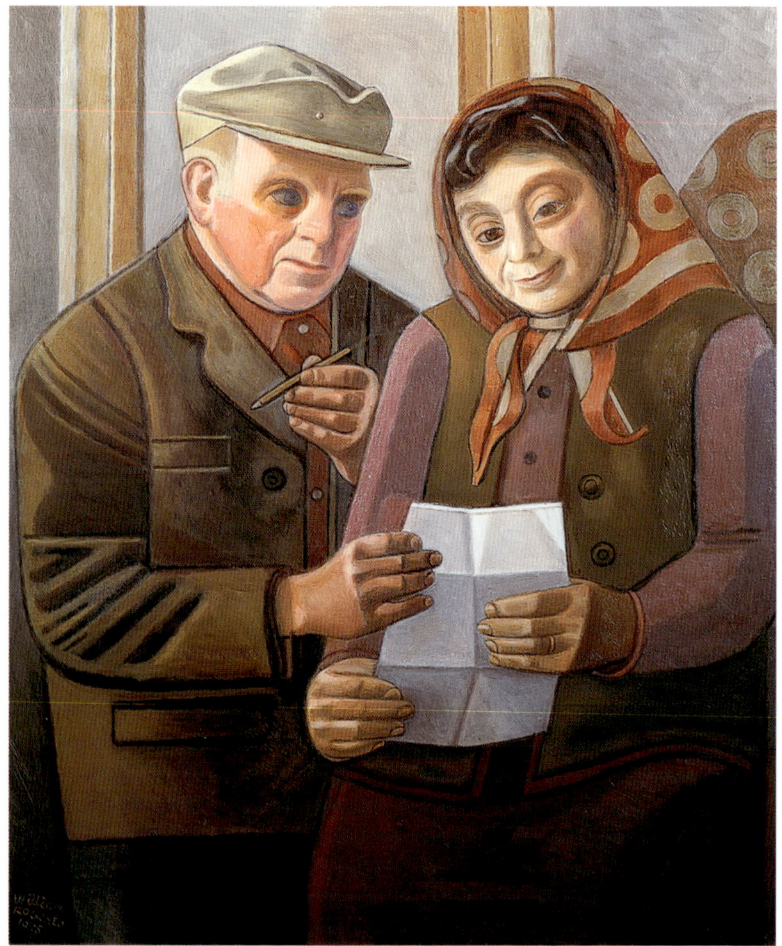

William Roberts
(1895–1980) and Sarah Roberts (1900–92), 1975

In 1922 William Roberts married Sarah Kramer, who was born in Leeds after her
family had come to England by boat from the Ukraine in 1900. Involved with the
Omega Workshops and Vorticism, Roberts developed his own rather Cubist style,
traces of which may still be discerned in this late work. His self-portrait centres on
a folded letter, perhaps a love letter to his beloved wife Sarah: there is a secret
complicity in their joint concentration.

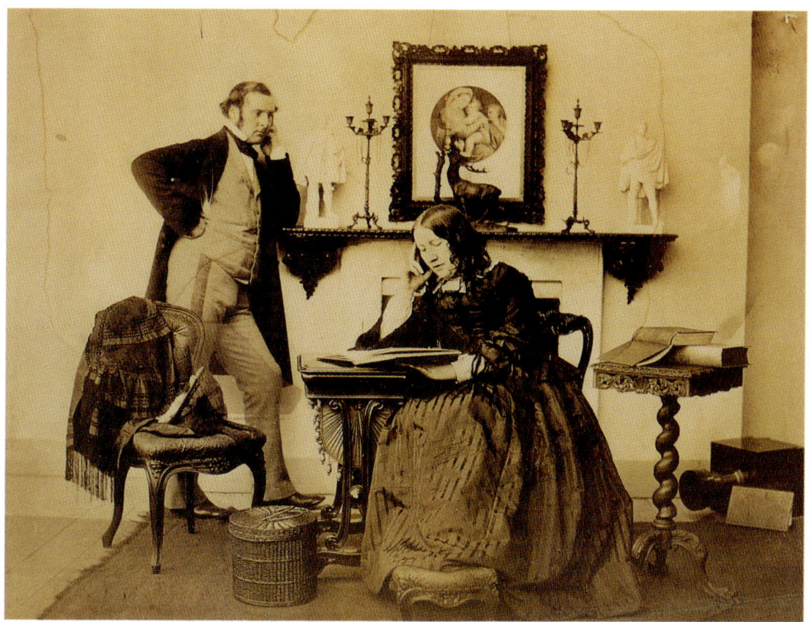

Benjamin Brecknell Turner (1815–94) with his wife Agnes Brecknell
Turner (1828–87), 1850s

A founder member of the Photographic Society of London, Brecknell
Turner used the calotype photographic process to make unusually large
paper negatives, up to 260 x 280mm (10¼ x 11") in size. This composition
is highly orchestrated: Agnes sits centrally, whilst Turner stands hand on
hip. As in Hayman's double portrait, the space is filled with possessions
that inform us about the pair. Also in prime position is a reproduction of
Raphael's *Madonna of the Chair* (Pitti Palace, Florence), an obviously
religious and artistic quotation, but perhaps also a reference to the
perceived primary role of women in Victorian times. To the right on the
floor lies a camera, included here in the same manner as a palette and
brushes in a painter's self-portrait.

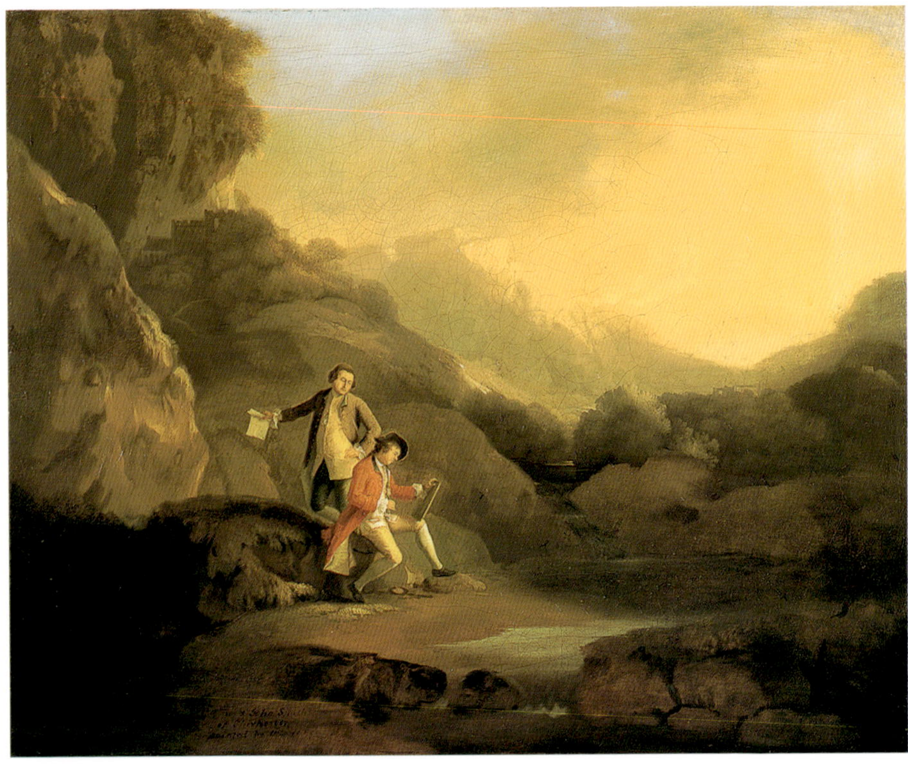

George Smith
(1713–76) with John Smith (1716/17–64), *c.*1760

The brothers George and John Smith worked in partnership, often on
the same canvas. They combined the study of reproductions of the
works of Claude and Poussin with their own observations taken
directly from nature using a camera obscura. Their double portrait,
in reflective poses, is a sympathetic rendering of their working
relationship.

Opposite:
John Hamilton Mortimer (1740–79) with a student, *c.*1765

Mortimer sits prominently, concentrating on a drawing, the folds of his
beautiful pale silk coat tumbling around a portfolio propped against
his chair. Everything in the painting is subsidiary to him, including his
student, whose eyes are lowered towards his master's drawing.
Mortimer painted conversation pieces and romantic subjects set in
the wild Italian countryside. President of the Society of Artists in 1774,
he died aged thirty-nine, just five years later.

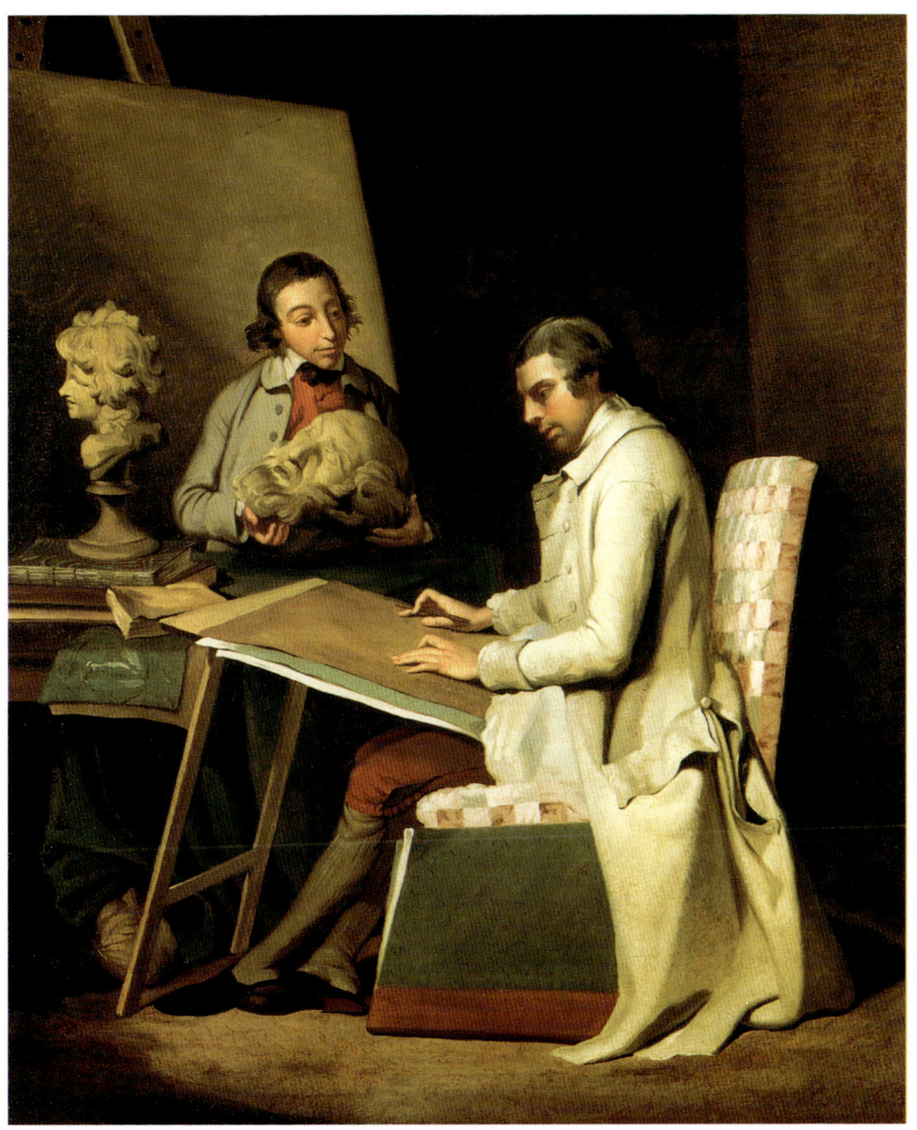

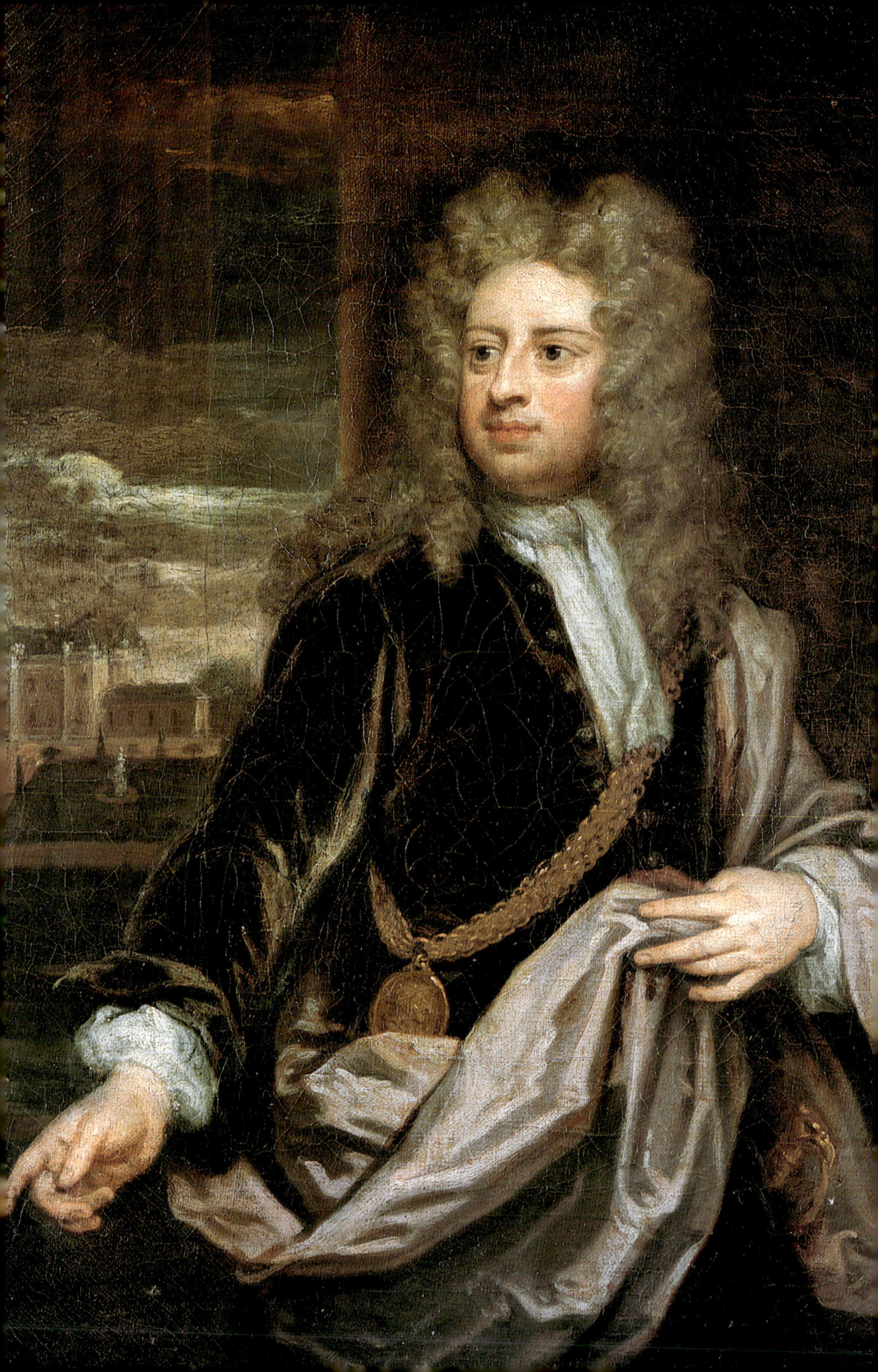

Chapter five
Symbols and signatures

Artists use symbols in all types of portraiture for communicating information about their sitters to the viewer. In self-portraiture artists may use familiar symbols, but they also personalise them. The significance of these references may get lost over time and teasing out their meaning can be an intriguing process; they may be so obscure or secret that the outsider never fully understands them. Sometimes, however, they are obvious: roses for love; children for fecundity and heritage; palettes and brushes denoting painting and creativity; cameras for photography; dogs represent faithful loyalty; and foods temporal plenty, with oysters as aphrodisiacs within this category.

The restrained English baroque of Sir Godfrey Kneller's self-portrait makes oblique reference to the gold chain in Sir Anthony van Dyck's *Self-portrait with a Sunflower* (*c.*1633; Collection of the Duke of Westminster; see Hollar's etched version on page 56). Artemisia Gentileschi (1593–1652/3) also wears a chain in her self-portrait as 'Pittura', the personification of the art of painting (1630; Royal Collection). This symbolism was derived from Cesare Ripa's book of moral emblems *Iconologia* (1593). Kneller's self-portrait is a useful example to consider as it encompasses references to politics, art and to success. The idea of visually paying homage to one's benefactor dates from Renaissance times. A self-portrait medal by Filarete (*c.*1460–66; Victoria and Albert Museum, London) has a Latin inscription that reads 'Just as the sun nurtures the bee, so the prince offers us preferment'. The bees are a metaphor for the industry and talent of the artist, and the sun by implication, the prince.

The Prague-born Wenceslaus Hollar's etching after Van Dyck's self-portrait of *c.*1633 belonging to King

Self-portraits

Sir Anthony van Dyck
(1599–1641), 1644

This etching by Wenceslaus
Hollar is based on Van Dyck's
Self-portrait with a Sunflower
(*c*.1633) – generally agreed to be
symbolic of Charles I's
patronage, which included a
knighthood on 5 July 1632, the
gift of a gold chain in 1633 and
a studio in Blackfriars. Van Dyck
was no stranger to etching and
himself produced a number of
original prints.

Charles I became a 'veritable symbol of the royalist
cause'. The importance of Van Dyck's work lies in the
fact that he was the creator of the enduring image of
the Caroline court, having been introduced to Charles
I by Rubens in whose studio he trained. Hollar
translated the reds and oranges in Van Dyck's portrait
through line and cross-hatchings to echo the tones and
form of the original, but he also changed the format
from rectangular to square in a radical departure from
the original – but still retaining the impact of this
striking composition. Van Dyck's influence on British
portraiture is undisputed: Thomas Gainsborough's
famously quoted last words – delivered over a
century later – were: 'We are all going to Heaven,
and Van Dyck is of the company'.

Henri Fantin-Latour in his *Homage to Delacroix*
(1864; Musée d'Orsay, Paris) in true romantic fashion
quotes his artistic allegiances by including himself in a

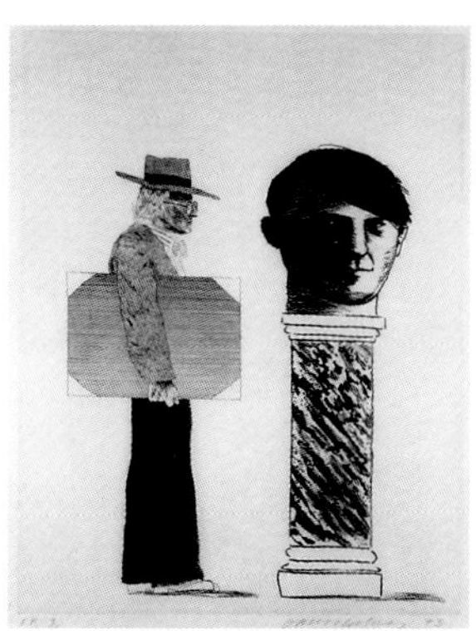

***The Student – Homage
to Picasso***
David Hockney (b.1937), 1973

Hockney, seen in profile, pays homage to his hero Picasso, whose 1960 retrospective at the Tate, London, had a significant impact on him. In 1974 Hockney produced another etching of them together entitled *Artist and Model* showing them seated opposite each other across a table. Hockney comments 'This etching is drawn from a photograph of Picasso, I would love to have met him, even just once.'

line-up that links him to renowned artistic and literary figures such as James Abbott McNeill Whistler, Charles Baudelaire, Édouard Manet and Eugène Delacroix.

David Hockney meanwhile pays homage to Picasso by showing him as a hero on a pedestal. There is something of a graphic similarity between the work of Hockney and that of William Hogarth 200 years earlier, not least because of both artists' commitment to drawing and printmaking. Hockney based his 1975 Glyndebourne Opera set designs for Igor Stravinsky's *Rake's Progress* on Hogarth's prints of 1735: 'I took the cross-hatching effect directly from Hogarth's engravings'. Interestingly, their self-portraits relate both in scale and specific detail. Hogarth's series of paintings such as *The Harlot's Progress* and *Marriage à la Mode* were popular and pirated, which led him to lobby for the passing of the Copyright Act. This was made law in 1735, and from then on artists' work was protected from unlawful reproduction. Francis Hayman (see page 47) was a friend of Hogarth's: they were both involved in the St Martin's Lane Academy, and they visited Calais together in 1748. The subtitle of Hogarth's souvenir image of this visit was *Les Rosbifs* (Tate, London): it includes a profile self-portrait similar to that illustrated on page 58 and confirms his own xenophobic stance – he portrays the French eating watery soup, while his own countrymen tuck in to beef!

Another great printmaker, the American James Abbott McNeill Whistler, transformed his signature into a symbol and the Whistler 'butterfly' became synonymous with his work, an early example of branding – to this day it is used as the logo of Chelsea Arts Club. With its connotations of transitory beauty, as a memento mori the butterfly is the perfect signature for self-portraiture.

Self-portraits

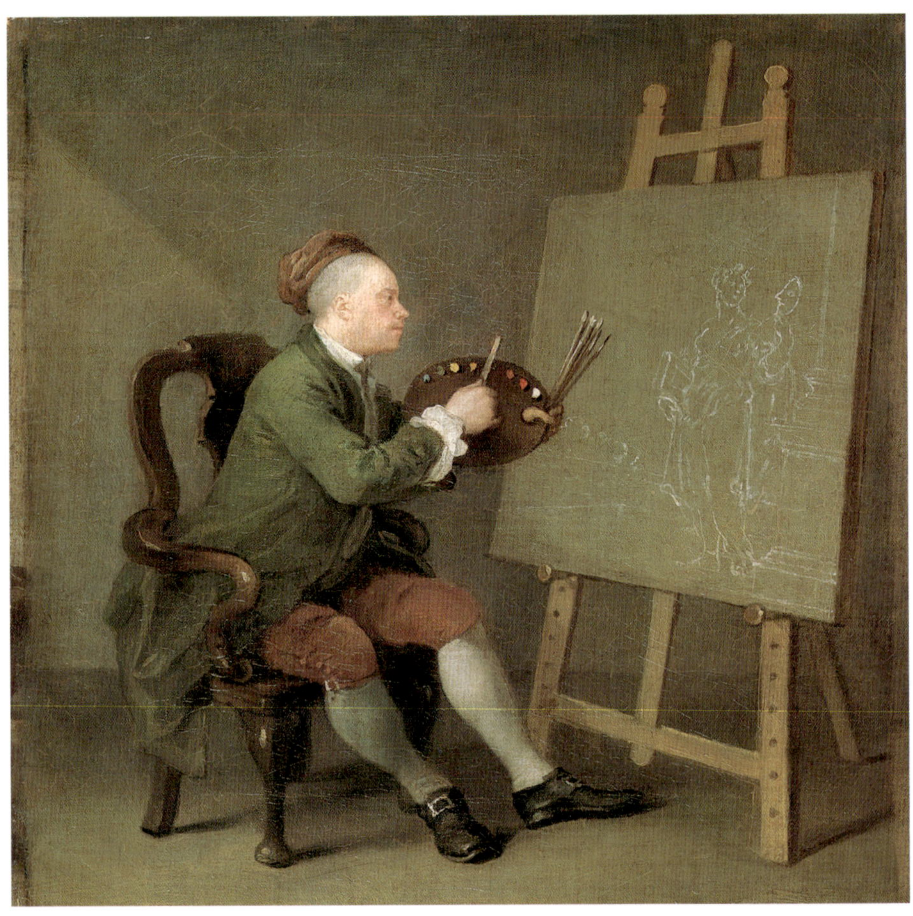

William Hogarth
(1697–1764), *c.*1757

Hogarth's painting is small, domestic in scale, and informative – he
demonstrates, for instance, how to organise paint, from light to dark
pigment, on his palette. On the grey ground of his canvas the white
outline of the Comic Muse is visible, the classical metaphor for the
inspiration behind his popular moralising series of satirical paintings
including *The Rake's Progress* and *Marriage à la Mode*.

Symbols and signatures

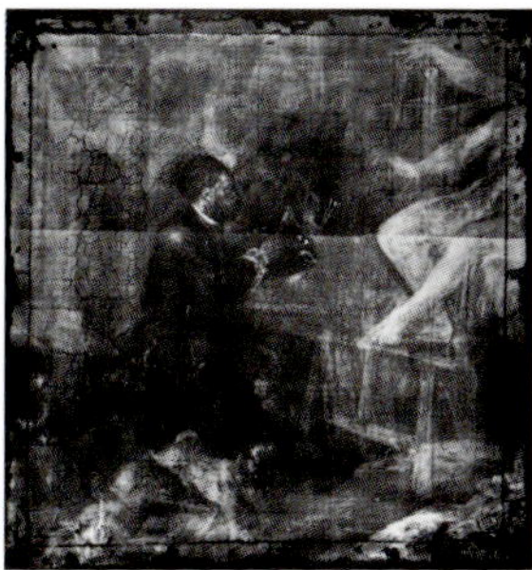

X-ray of William Hogarth's self-portrait of *c*.1757

In Hogarth's theoretical treatise *The Analysis of Beauty* (1753) he makes his prejudice against foreign artists very clear. This X-ray of the painting shows his pug Crabb, successor to Trump, the dog featured in Hogarth's self-portrait of the 1750s (Tate, London), relieving himself on two framed paintings presumed to be by foreign artists. It has been suggested that Hogarth's appointment as Serjeant Painter to His Majesty in 1757 provoked this change of composition.

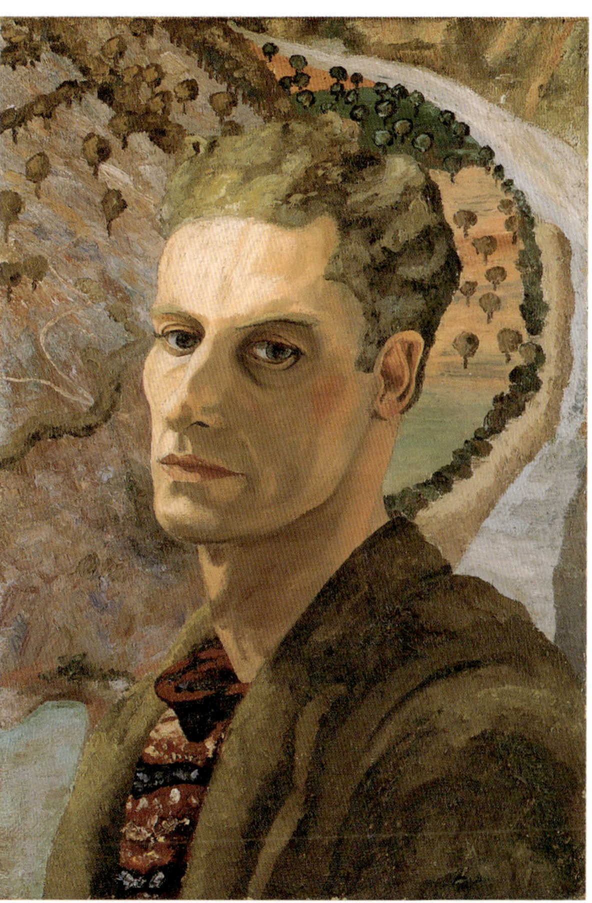

Sir Cedric Lockwood Morris
(1889–1982), *c*.1930

Morris left London with his companion Arthur Lett-Haines in 1937. They founded an art school together in Dedham, Suffolk, re-establishing it in Benton End after a fire. The prospectus talked about training 'sincere' artists who could work in 'freedom': famous alumni include Lucian Freud and Maggi Hambling. The landscape backdrop in this painting is symbolic of Morris's love of nature. He was a keen breeder of irises and a pioneer of hand-pollination – several species of irises and geraniums still bear his name. The serpentine line of the undulating river echoes his elegant chiselled features.

Self-portraits

Sir George Frampton
(1860–1928), 1894

Frampton was a scholar and a craftsman who was involved in the Arts and Crafts movement. His elegant and patriotic stone memorial to Edith Cavell, executed for her part in helping Allied soldiers to escape from Brussels in 1915, stands opposite the main entrance to the National Portrait Gallery in St Martin's Place. His signature is carved at its base, together with the date, 1920, in similar style to his pencil self-portrait here, which is inscribed 'Geo Frampton by himself Jan 1894'. The format of this self-portrait echoes Holbein's portraits.

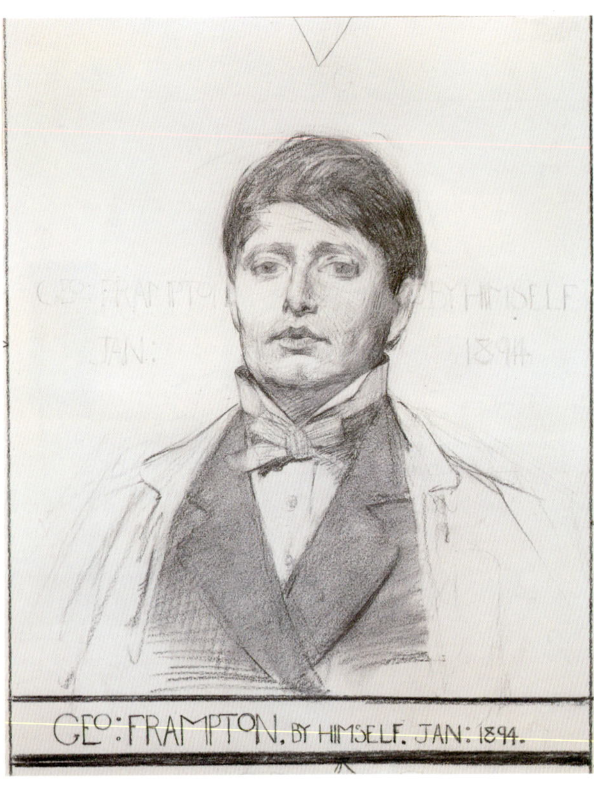

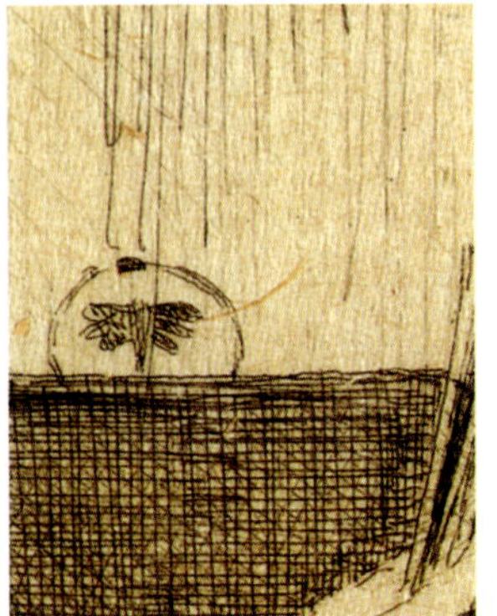

Opposite and left (detail):
James Abbott McNeill Whistler (1834–1903), 1874

This print is based on Whistler's *Arrangement in Grey: Portrait of the Painter* (c.1872; Detroit Institute of Arts). There are at least twenty different forms of his signature: here the butterfly motif occurs on a horizon line behind the artist. He repeats this format in *Arrangement in Grey and Black, no.2: Thomas Carlyle* (1872–3; Glasgow Museums and Art Galleries). Whistler's first dated butterfly was drawn in 1869 and was derived from a monogram of his initials. Monogram signatures are more common than symbolic motifs, and became particularly fashionable with Art Nouveau artists of the nineteenth century.

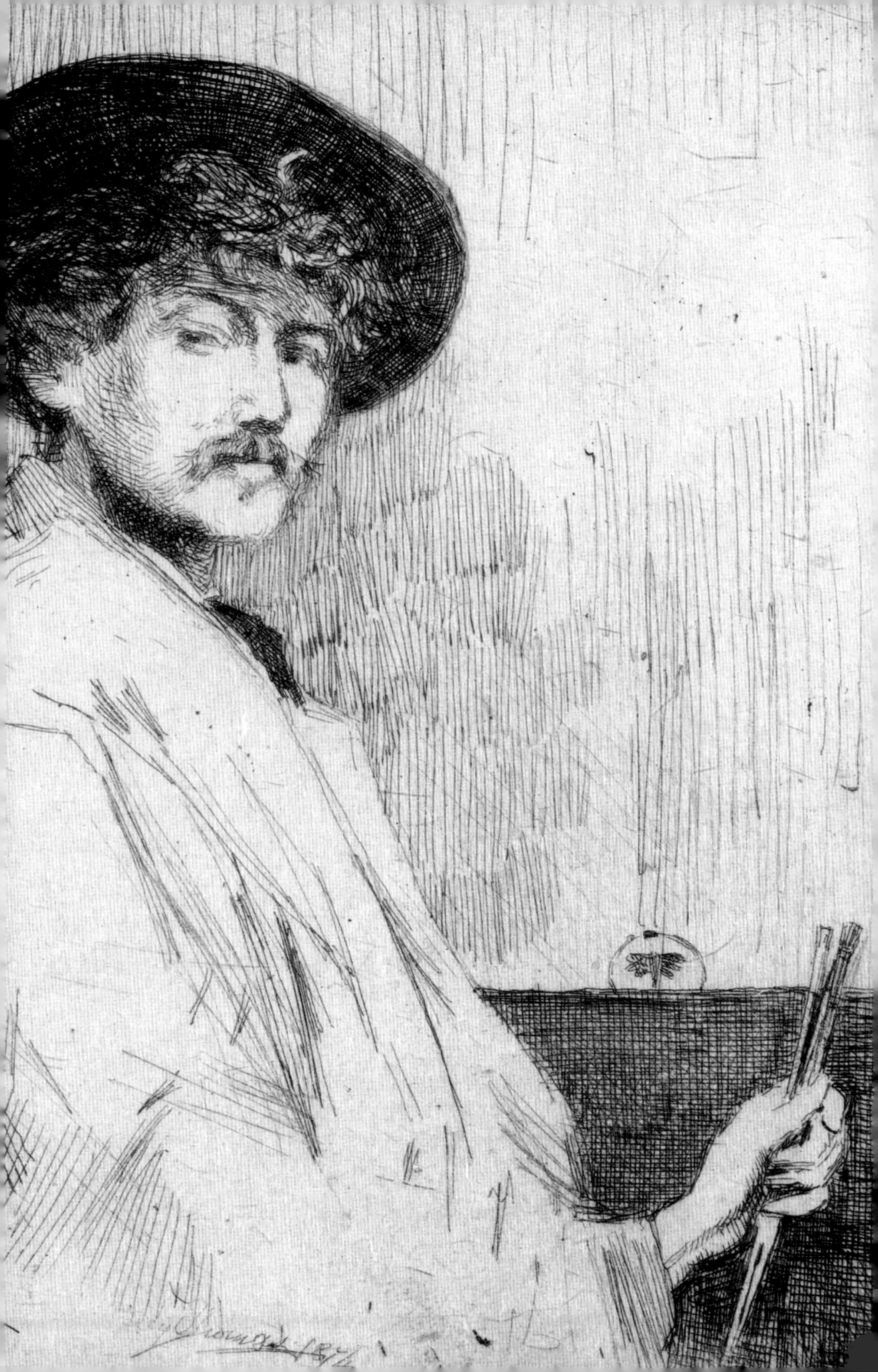

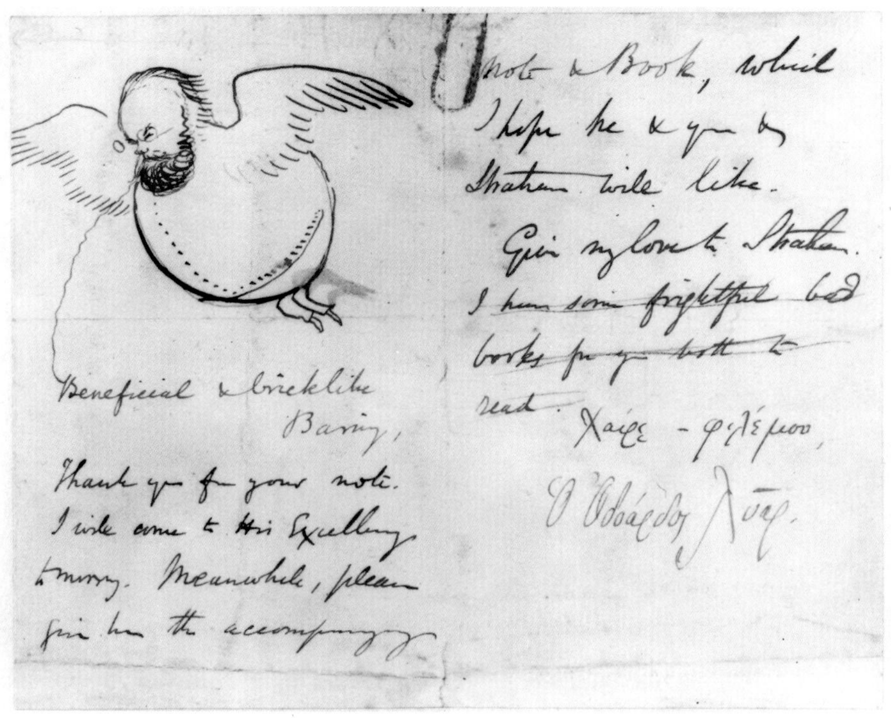

Edward Lear
(1812–88), 1864

Lear's self-image as pot-bellied birdman is self-deprecatory, typically whimsical and one that he used again in 1872. Combining word and image, he incorporates his signature and self-portrait into a letter, thus conflating the two and recalling Sir Francis Chantrey's drawing (page 80). As an antidote to his more serious work as a landscape watercolourist, Lear wrote and illustrated books of nonsense poems.

Opposite:
John Havinden
(1908–87), 1930

Havinden's work as a photographer was modernist: stark, abstract and uncompromising. Time working at his brother's design company perhaps inspired the clever fusion of sans-serif type with the shape of his glasses. Havinden's self-portrait alludes to *Foto-Auge (Photo-Eye)*, a book published in Germany in 1929 to mark the Stuttgart 'Film und Foto' exhibition.

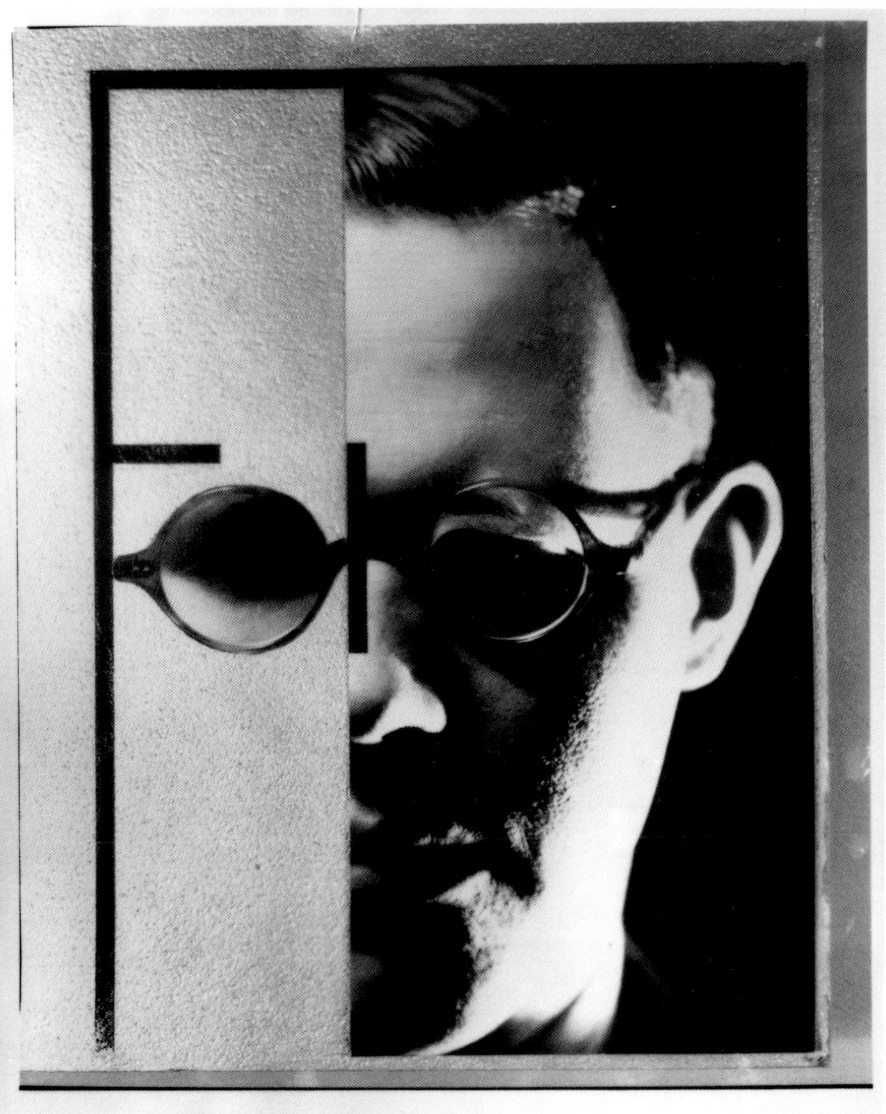

Self-portraits

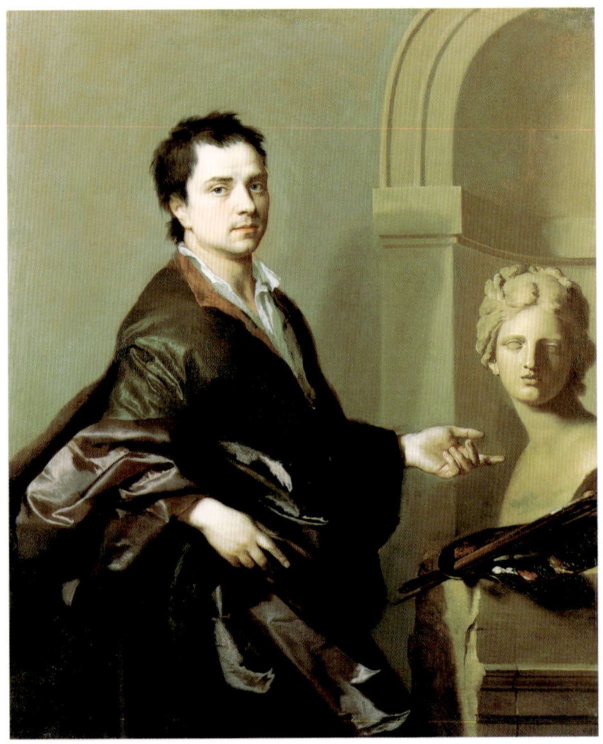

Michael Dahl
(*c*.1659–1743), 1691

Michael Dahl came to England from Stockholm in 1682. He travelled
to Paris in 1685 and then to Rome, where he painted Queen Kristina
of Sweden before returning to England in 1689. George Vertue
described him as 'a man of great modesty and few words'. In this
self-portrait Dahl's short hair, cut in Ancient Roman style, both echoes
his surroundings and emphasises his intellectual aspirations. Lest we
forget that his primary objective is the creation of beauty, he gestures
towards a symbolic bust of the Medici Venus, below which his palette
and brushes rest.

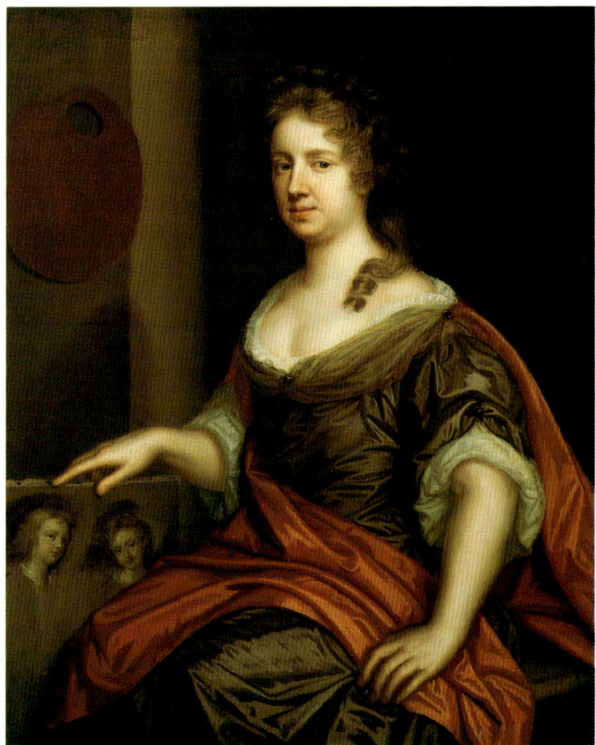

Mary Beale
(1633–99), *c*.1665

Mary Beale's self-portrait is a succinct statement of her dual role as mother and painter. Like Hogarth, she uses the trope of a painting within the painting. In her hand she holds an unfinished painting of her two sons, Charles and Bartholomew, while her palette hangs on the wall behind. Mary's husband, Charles, ran the studio as book-keeper and colourman, referring to her fondly as 'Dear heart' in his sitter and account books. He had trained as a painter, but recognising his wife's superior talent, focused his efforts on managing the business. A successful portrait painter, Mary augmented her own list of sitters thanks to her friend Sir Peter Lely, who would sometimes recommend clients to her.

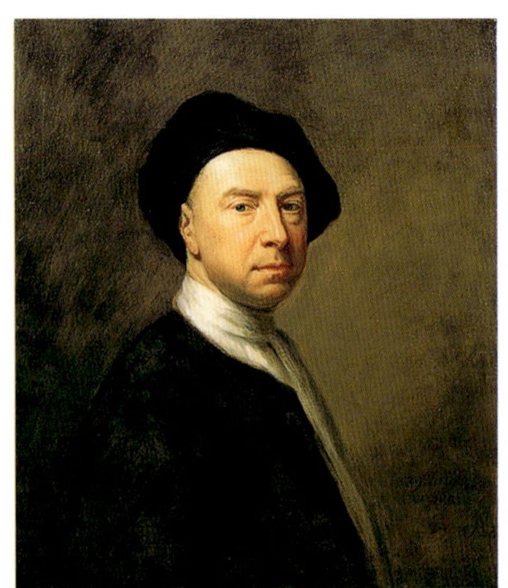

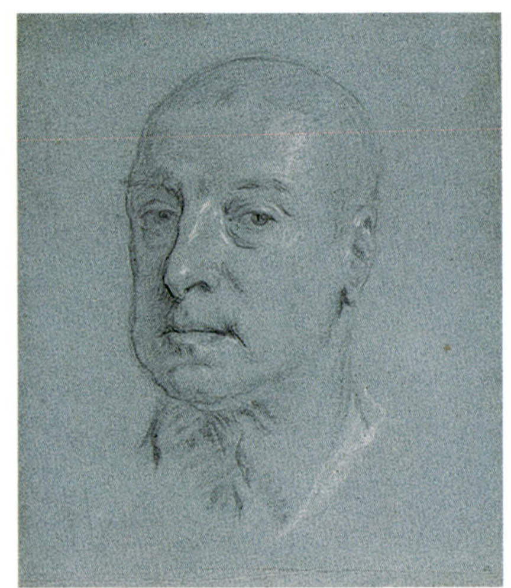

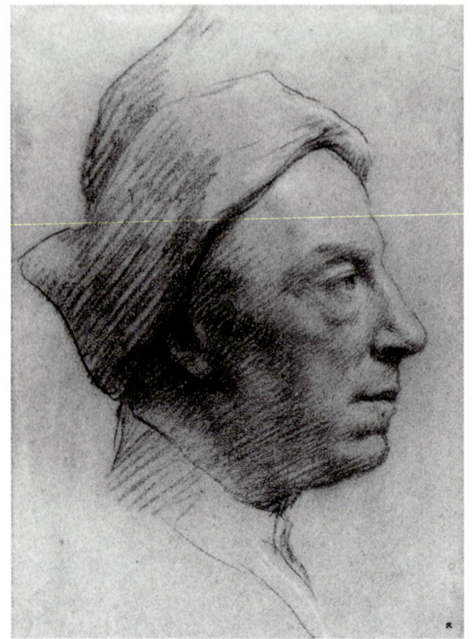

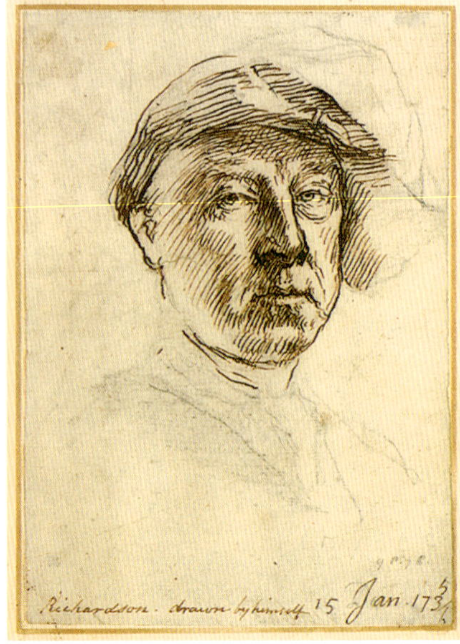
Richardson. drawn by himself 15 Jan 173 5/4

Dated October 1735, when Richardson was sixty-eight years old, the black chalk image with white highlights (top right) is a candid self-scrutiny. Wigless, he is undressed, presenting his bare and bony bald pate together with the crêpy folds of his neck skin. It is a startlingly different self-perspective to the other three more conventional views. Richardson is recognisable in all, the varying media and poses illustrating his propensity to use self-portraiture as a means of flexing his artistic muscles.

Chapter six
Getting older

Over the course of their careers, artists will invariably be aware of their changing appearance and impending mortality – and some come to maintain a dialogue with the Vanitas theme that runs as a thread through their work. Successive self-portraits by an artist over a long career may chart his or her physical as well as artistic development; added to that, the certainty of eventual death means that each self-portrait, in the eyes of its maker, may be the last.

For Jonathan Richardson, self-portraiture was a way of life. His *Essay on the Theory of Painting* (1715), which contains perceptive statements about the notion of being an artist, is a written form of self-portrait. He states that 'In Picture we never die, never decay, or grow older.' Horace Walpole, who attended the sale of Richardson's renowned collection of Old Master drawings, recorded that Richardson made daily portraits of himself and his son after he retired. This enabled him to document their changing physiognomies in the context of their familial likeness.

Physical imprints of longevity, character and inherited features can be traced though self-portraits by other artists since Richardson, and through comparing the works of artists from the same family. In the case of William and Ben Nicholson, for example, or the prolific Pissarro family, who painted themselves and each other over more than a century, family traits can be traced from one portrait to another.

Rembrandt is perhaps the most famous producer of the 'ageing self-portrait'. Compare, for instance, his two self-portraits in the National Gallery, London: we are familiar with his clear-eyed confident and richly dressed image of 1640, aged thirty-four, deliberately emulating the portraits of Raphael, Dürer and Titian. In his later self-portrait of 1669, made in the year of

Self-portraits

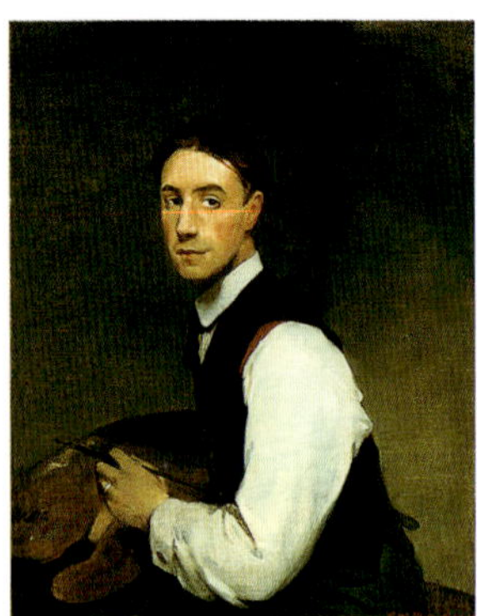

Glyn Philpot
(1884–1937), 1908

This is Philpot's only known painted self-portrait, so for us he will remain twenty-four years old, 'forever young'. Signed and dated 1908, this work was only exhibited once during his lifetime, in 1909, and shows him fresh-faced, handsome and ambitious, seated with his palette half-turned towards the viewer. Initially successful painting society portraits, his work fell from favour around 1932 when he moved to Paris and turned to Cubism. Philpot here pays tribute to his artistic hero Velázquez with his exquisite brushwork and subtle use of blacks and greys.

his death, his physical and artistic presence reflects the sea change in his fortune. This is well documented; but external fortunes alone were not the only reason for the evolution of his work. His concerns as an artist have also evolved: the quality of his paint-encrusted canvas surface now seems to suggest an ever-deepening spirituality.

It is said that the eye is the window to the soul, mirroring emotions and feelings. With its propensity for developing crow's feet and sagging skin, it can of course also betray our age. William Hogarth is pragmatic in *The Analysis of Beauty* (1753). He clearly outlines the reasons why our features sag, saying: 'It is by the natural and unaffected movements of the muscles, caused by the passions of the mind, that every man's character would in some measure be written in his face, by the time he arrives at forty years of age'. He continues by lamenting the 'further havoc time continues to make after the age of fifty'. The figurative self-portrait can reveal the visible effects of ageing – the increase in jowls, wrinkles and so forth – or it can discreetly gloss over the truth. Photographs on the other hand, even when retouched, can be cruel in their absolute accuracy. The pioneering photographer Madame Yevonde's self-portraits are humbling (see pages 74–5). She is candid and honest, wobbly and fragile, and always gloriously defiant.

Another aspect of ageing, which frequently emerges through self-portraiture, is that of self-challenging by the artist, continuing to focus on issues of self-evaluation and introspection over the passing of the years. These primary anxieties, specific to the individual, persist despite increasing age and experience – whether or not they are honestly reflected in art.

Artists who live a long time can also serve as mentors to new generations, their creativity stimulated by living through historic events and being able to

Getting older

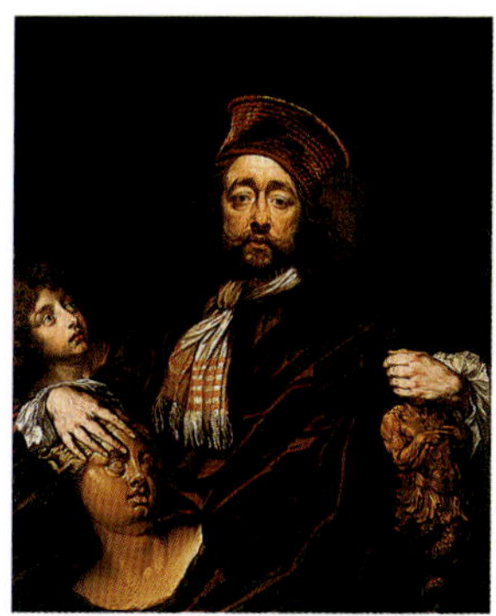

Isaac Fuller
(1606?–72), *c*.1670

A decorative and portrait painter, Fuller produced the earliest British drawing book (1654), a copy of which is in the British Museum. He trained in France and was in England after 1650, working in Oxford and London.

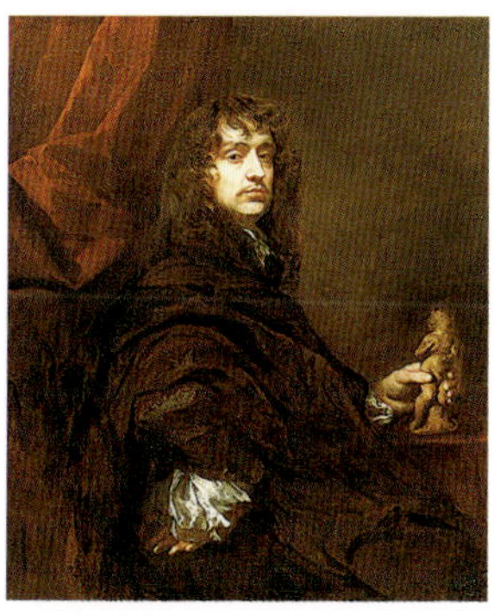

Sir Peter Lely
(1618–80), *c*.1660

Lely was both a portrait painter and an art collector. He came to London from Holland in the 1640s and worked throughout the Civil War and interregnum. In 1660 he was formally appointed Principal Painter to Charles II.

experiment with new discoveries. Walter Sickert, who died at the age of eighty-two, was instrumental in changing attitudes towards the use of photography in painting. With the use of basic gridlines he would transpose newspaper imagery onto canvas, a method that lent immediacy and energy to the results. Glyn Philpot defied the ravages of time by leaving only one self-portrait to posterity, painted when he was just twenty-four years old.

Over the years artists develop their work and become more confident. The countless self-portraits by Angus McBean and Cecil Beaton are a fine illustration of their evolving relaxed and inventive attitude towards photography. Kneller's self-portrait testifies to his success and material wealth; an updated version of his portrait in the Uffizi Collection, Florence, now incorporates a view of his new home Whitton Hall. In contrast to the elegant mondanity of Kneller's view of himself, Isaac Fuller leaves us a robust and positively raffish image, which seems to confirm reports of a life of dissipation. His contemporary Sir Peter Lely bemoaned his fate: 'that so great a genius should besot or neglect so great a talent'.

Walter Sickert
(1860–1942), 1930

Sickert depicts himself aged seventy, in a large-check tweed suit, bowler hat and walking stick. The abrupt composition, with figures caught in motion, of this thin grisaille painting shows its origins in the huge collection of torn-out press photos that Sickert assembled and which were the basis of much of his late work. Sickert trained at the Slade, and is best known for his depictions of music hall entertainments and urban life.

Opposite:
Jo Spence
(1934–92), 1990

Spence's self-portrait is confrontational: she appears deliberately grotesque, her face hidden behind a hag-like mask. Armed with a knife and a shield, she is both frightening and comical: the inclusion of chocolates is a further surreal element. Spence's work was political, investigative and often collaborative. Seen as a feminist, she would parody and rarely flatter the female form in her art. She pioneered what she called 'Phototherapy', a method of photographic visualisation that she used in her fight against breast cancer; she eventually succumbed to the disease at the age of fifty-eight.

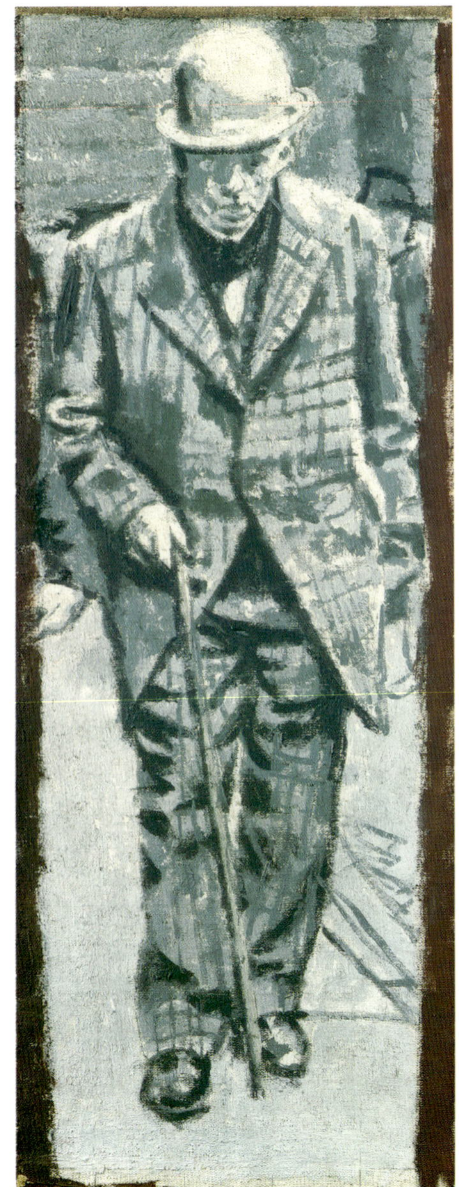

Getting older

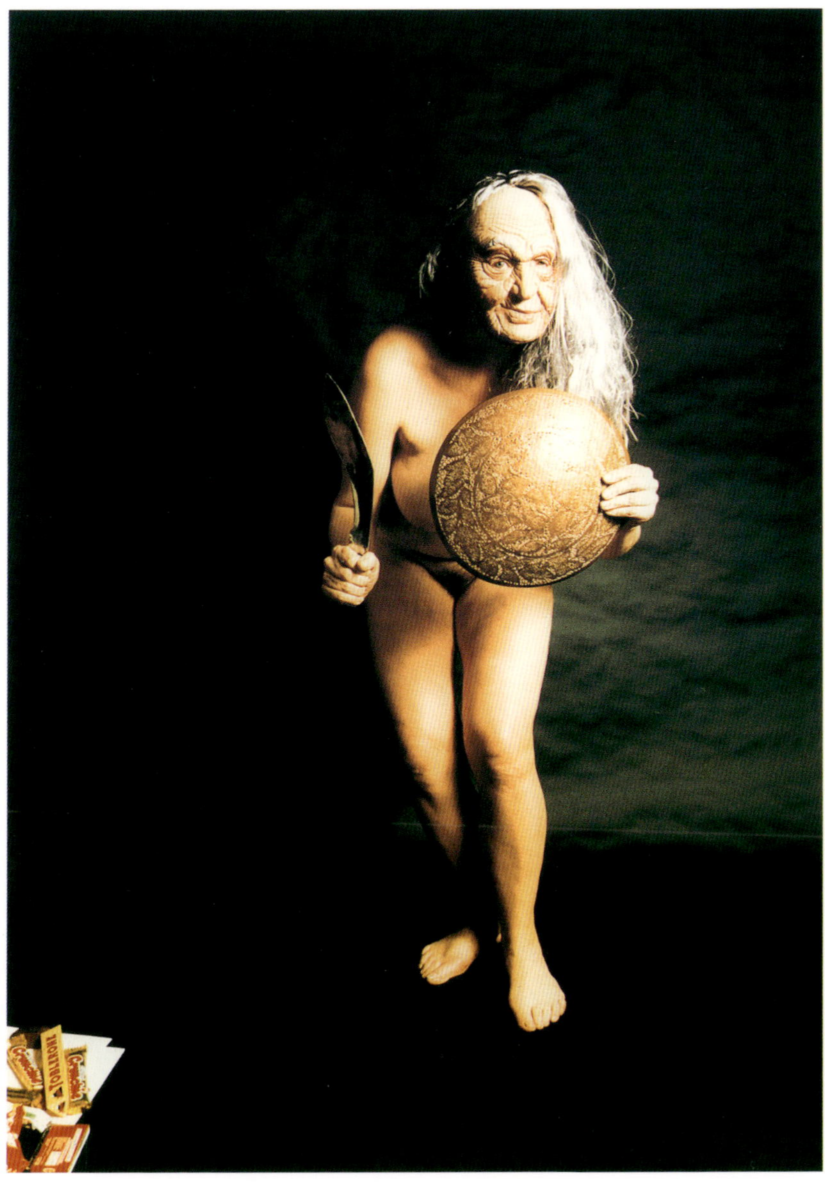

Dorothy Wilding
(1893–1976), 1920s

Queen of style, Wilding was the
most fashionable photographer
of her time, running chic studios
in both London and New York.
During the 1930s she favoured
clean lines and used minimalist
white blocks as settings for her
sitters. Her clients included
royalty, film stars such as
Yul Brynner, Cary Grant and
Tallulah Bankhead, and artists
such as the Zinkeisen sisters
(see pages 33 and 41). Shown
here in her thirties, she presents
a demure profile wearing pearls,
her head slightly tilted upwards,
conveying an impression
of hope.

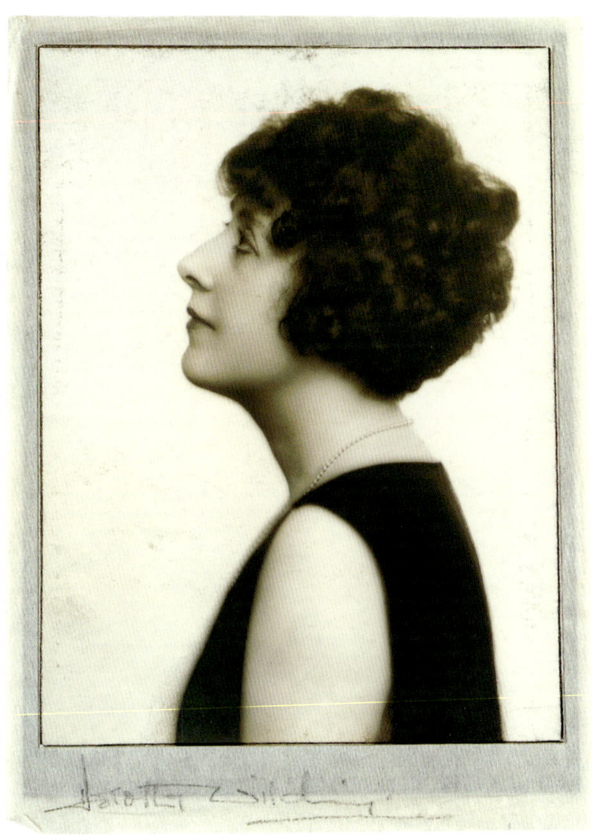

Opposite:
Dorothy Wilding
1956

Now aged sixty-three, Wilding tangibly radiates personality: a
glorious grin, zany glasses and impressive jewellery confirm her
enduringly positive attitude towards life. Two years later, in 1958,
her autobiography *In Pursuit of Perfection* was published; she
then retired.

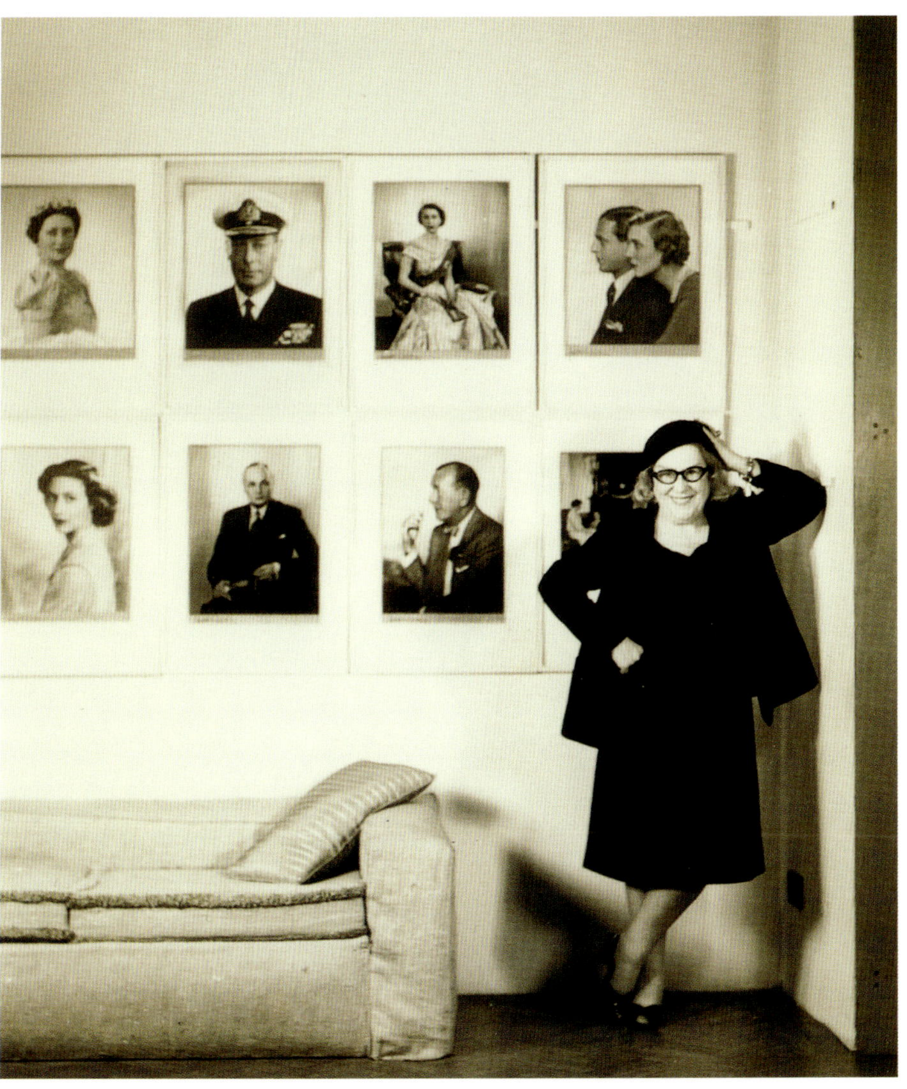

Self-portraits

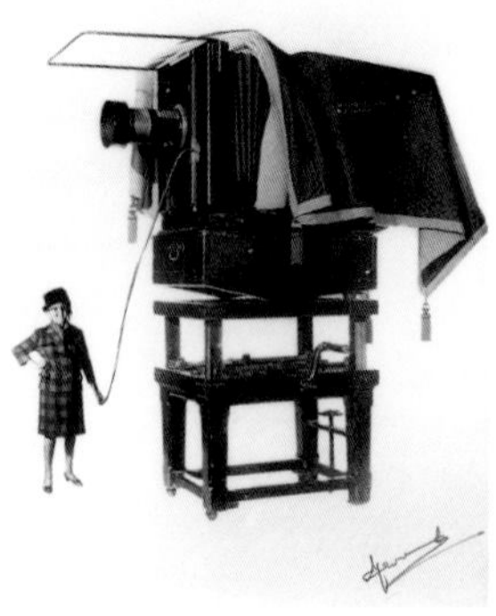

Madame Yevonde
(1893–1975), 1967

Yevonde's mantra was 'Be original or die' – and she was highly original. A dynamic artist and a consummate businesswoman, she possessed an eye for detail and positively delighted in the challenge of new processes, particularly that of colour photography. Her extravagant use of colour and symbolism, with surrealist flair, can be seen in her famous 'Goddesses', a series of portraits of society beauties inspired by the charity Olympian ball held at Claridges in 1935. This image, taken when Yevonde was seventy-four, was used as the cover for *Some Distinguished Women: Photographs by Yevonde*, 1968.

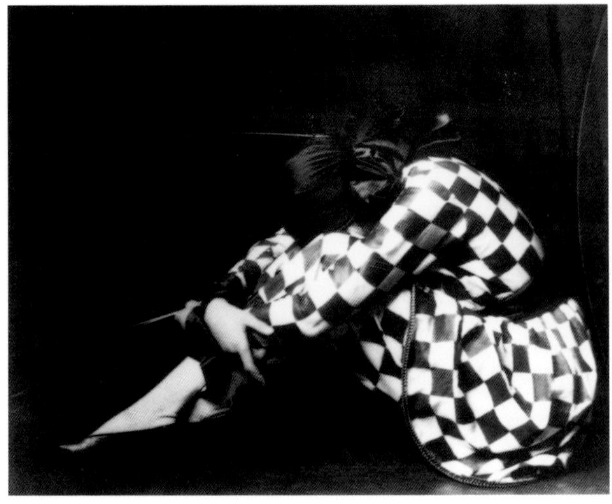

Madame Yevonde
1925

Yevonde presents herself as a harlequin in this self-portrait taken when she was thirty-two years old. Seated on the floor, she hides her face from the camera, allowing the pattern to take centre stage, an uncharacteristically modest pose.

Opposite:
Madame Yevonde
1970

Always in the avant-garde, Yevonde's self-portraits aged seventy-four and seventy-seven show a woman honest about the ageing process and confident about communicating the important tools of her trade. The focus on lighting and the foregrounding of camera equipment dominate, while she records her own courage in the face of physical decline. In comparing these self-portraits with the modest, secretive image she made when she was thirty-two, a visible connection emerges: the distinctive black-and-white chequered cloth that acts as a trademark and seems loudly to proclaim her four-square good sense and indomitable spirit.

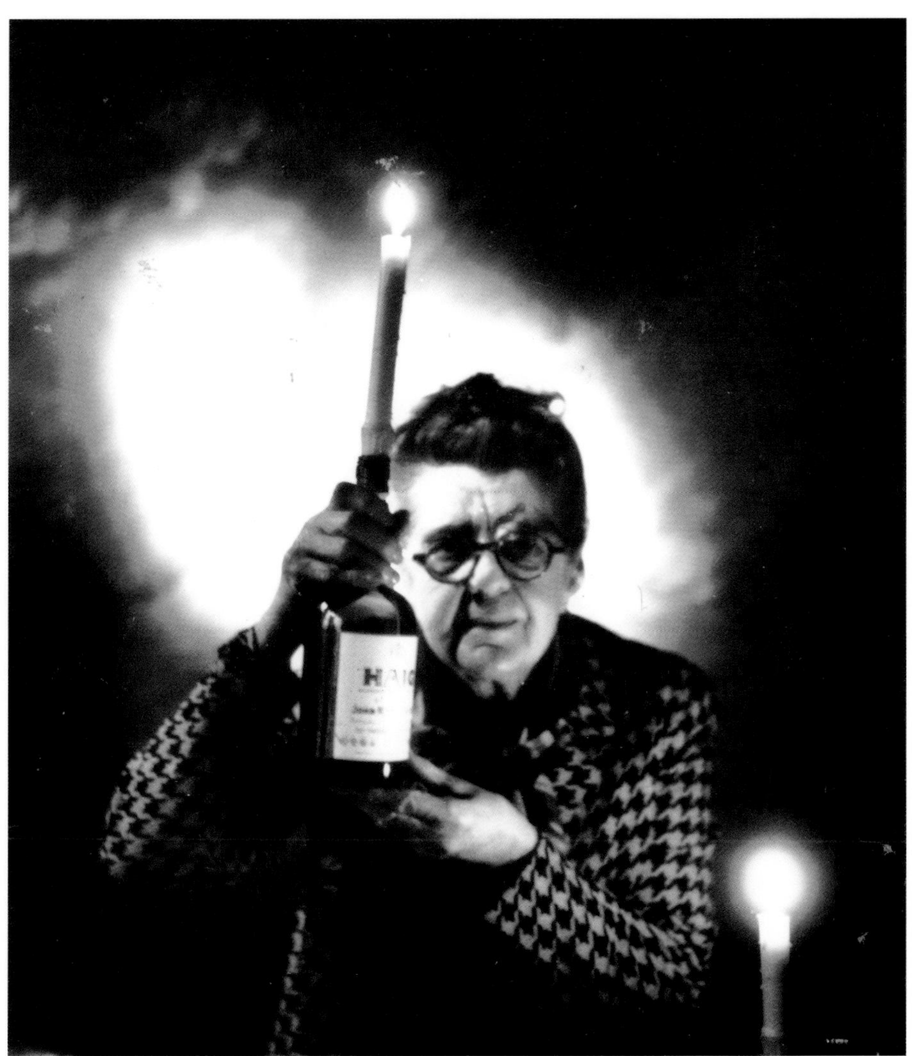

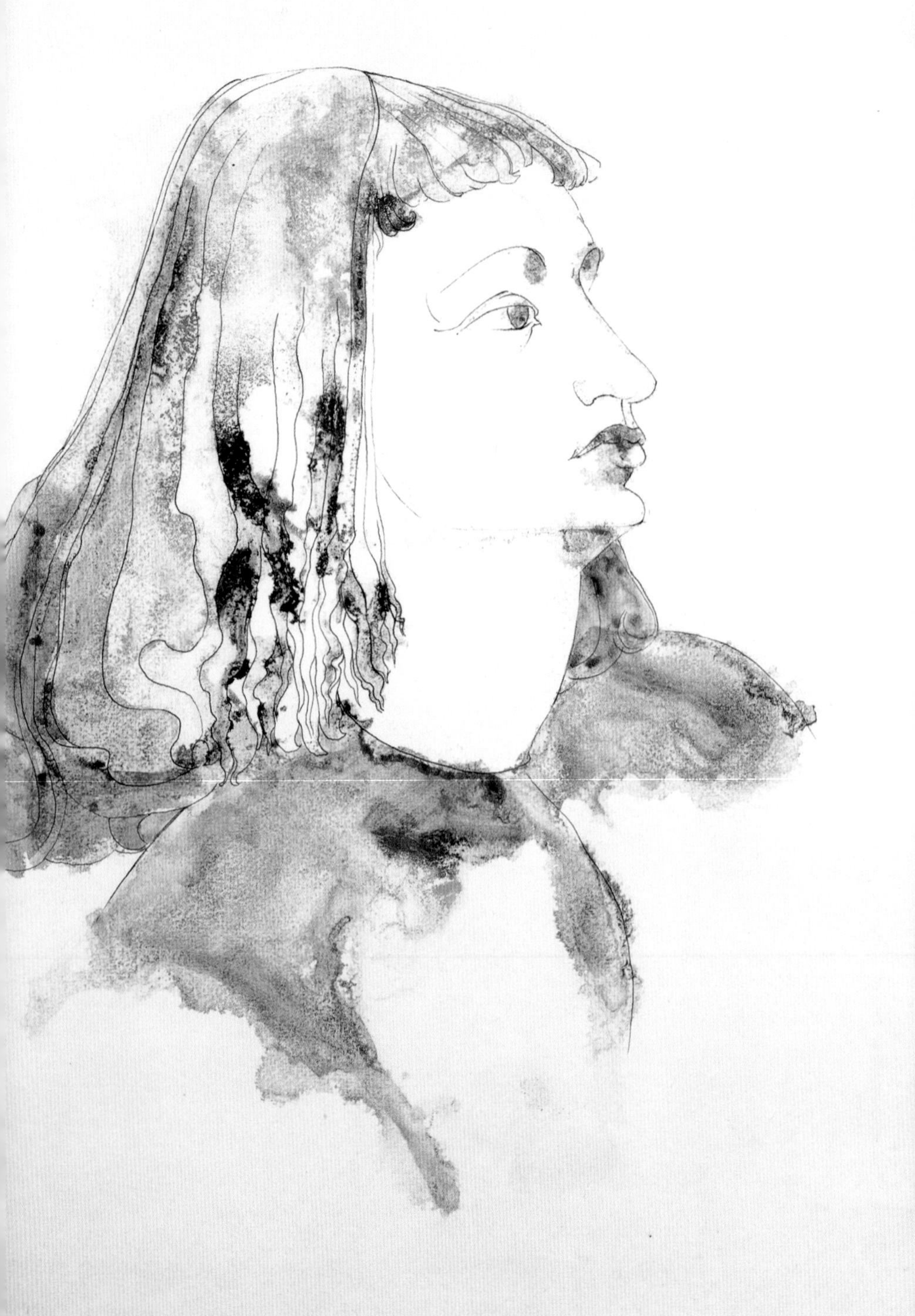

Chapter seven
Portraying the psyche

Staring at your reflection in a mirror is one form of self-examination: if done for long enough, you may start meditating on your own psyche. This gives us a taste of the challenges facing the self-portrait artist: how to convey complexities of personality and talent while at the same time reflecting layers of conscious emotion and personal history. The portraits in this section reveal aspects of the artists' subconscious, of which they themselves may have been unaware, even perhaps, for instance, their impact on their own environment. Could Lucian Freud's paint-encrusted studio walls be likened to a subconscious portrait, as a literal record of the paint he uses in his work? Francis Bacon's studio has been preserved, lifted in its entirety from Kensington to Dublin, where it stands as a memorial to the painter, a physical narrative encapsulating his complex real and subconscious life.

Jung's theory of a collective unconsciousness has led to widespread research into the psychology of artists and whether they are more susceptible to depression or obsession because of their chosen profession. Certainly a substantial number of artists feel alienated from society. Michael Ayrton refers to a 'great maze which is my life' in his novel *The Maze Maker* (1967), the fictional autobiography of the mythical Greek architect and inventor Daedalus, who designed the maze to imprison the Minotaur in Knossos, Crete, and made wax wings for Icarus. The concept of the labyrinth has long preoccupied and stimulated the creative imaginations of artists and writers, standing as a metaphor for the workings of the brain, the organ that instigates creativity, giving form to abstract explorations and trying to organise perceptions of the microcosm and macrocosm of this world: who am I and why am I here?

Ithell Colquhoun
(1906–88), 1930s

Artist and writer Colquhoun was associated with Surrealism, Automatism and the Occult. She used her imaginative compositions to explore dreams and the subconscious. This image is one of two from the same sitting that suggest the use of complex mirror arrangements, perhaps reflecting a 'duality of life'. Two views of the sitter taken at the same time also provoke an idea of alternate aspects of a personality, and its interpretation by different people at different times in different moods.

Self-portraits

John Tunnard's self-portrait harks back to Robert Hooke's *Micrographia* (1665), a hugely popular and influential book that showed magnified drawings from natural history for the first time and allowed people to view the world of creation in detail. A keen naturalist, Tunnard's speciality was sawflies; in his self-portrait his glasses take on the shape of a fly's eyes, whilst his head echoes the form of its thorax. This surreal image taps into our fascination with the unknown and uncontrollable, a theme hinted at by Tunnard in discussing his methods:

> I sometimes begin a drawing with no preconceived problem to solve ... with no conscious aim; but as my mind takes in what is so produced a point arrives where some idea becomes conscious and crystallises ... .

Both Sir Francis Chantrey and Sir George Scharf represent ironic views of their own difficult, if temporary, situations. Their humour reveals a lack of pomposity with regard to their status and also their utterly obsessive need to keep drawing whatever the circumstances. Ithell Colquhoun used fluid ink and wash in her self-portrait to evoke a magical, dreamlike quality, a world away from the comic drawings of Chantrey and Scharf.

The self-portrait is an ongoing conundrum for the artist. Lowry said 'In all those heads of the late thirties I was trying to make them as grim as possible. I reflected myself in those pictures ... they were all based on myself.' And of his self-portrait, 'I thought, "What's the use of it? I don't want it and nobody else will." I seemed to want to make it as grotesque as possible.'

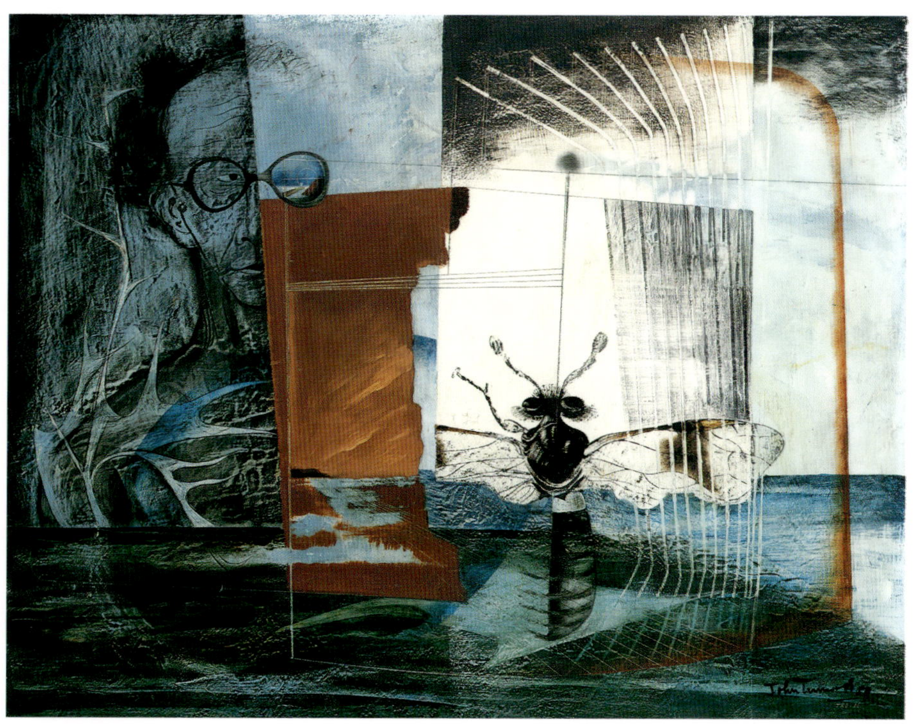

John Tunnard
(1900–71), 1959

Tunnard felt that it was important to paint 'from the stomach as well as the head'. In 1939 he sold a painting to Peggy Guggenheim, who likened his appearance to Groucho Marx. Like Reynolds, Tunnard draws attention to the artist's most important asset – the eyes – by retaining his glasses.

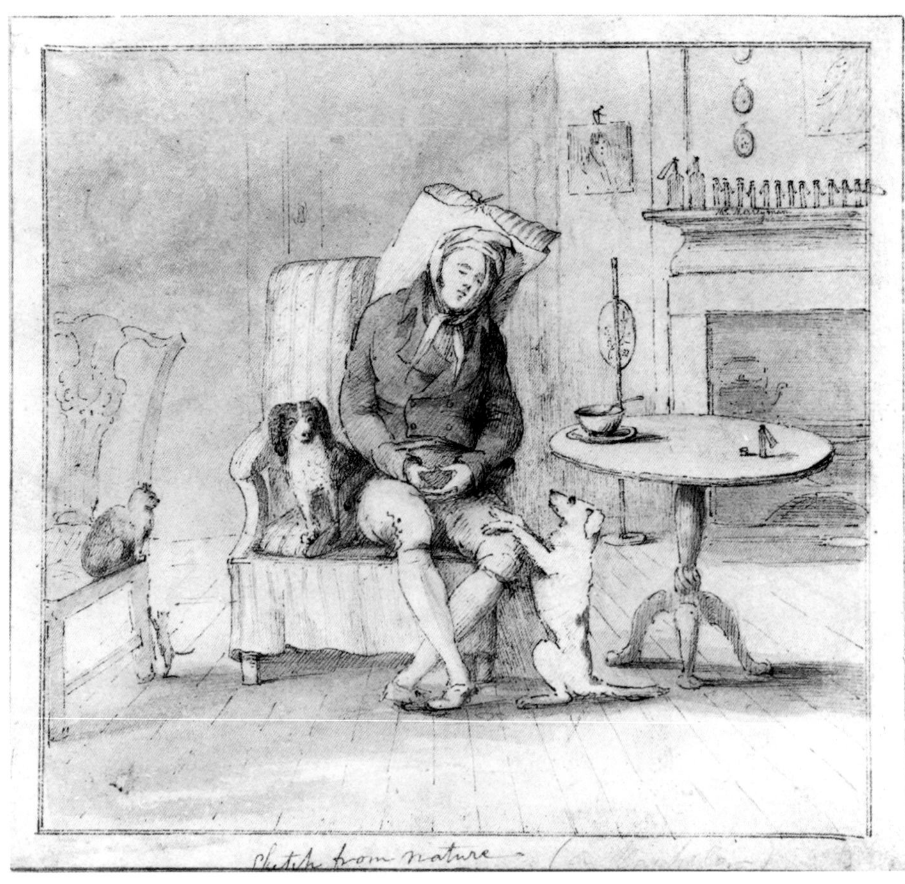

Sir Francis Leggatt Chantrey (1781–1841), *c*.1800

Chantrey's self-mocking drawing recalls that of Edward Lear (page 62), and is an apology note for his absence from a dinner date with friends due to mumps. According to a contemporary account, the labelled medicine bottles were intended to spell out the name of his doctor, Dr Merreman. The patient's expression is not 'merry' and his retinue of pets are so concerned that they ignore the potential fun of a visiting mouse. Virtually self-taught and known for his 'speaking likenesses', Chantrey came from poverty in Sheffield to London, where he sculpted portrait busts, including commissions for statues of King George III (1811; Guildhall) and George IV (1829; Trafalgar Square).

Sir George Scharf
(1820–95), 1869

In 1857 the National Portrait
Gallery was opened at 29 Great
George Street, Westminster,
and Scharf was appointed
Secretary. He led the Gallery's
subsequent moves to
Kensington in 1870 and to
Bethnal Green in 1885, having
become Director in 1882. His
drawing wittily exaggerates the
uncertainties of the Gallery's
potential homelessness.

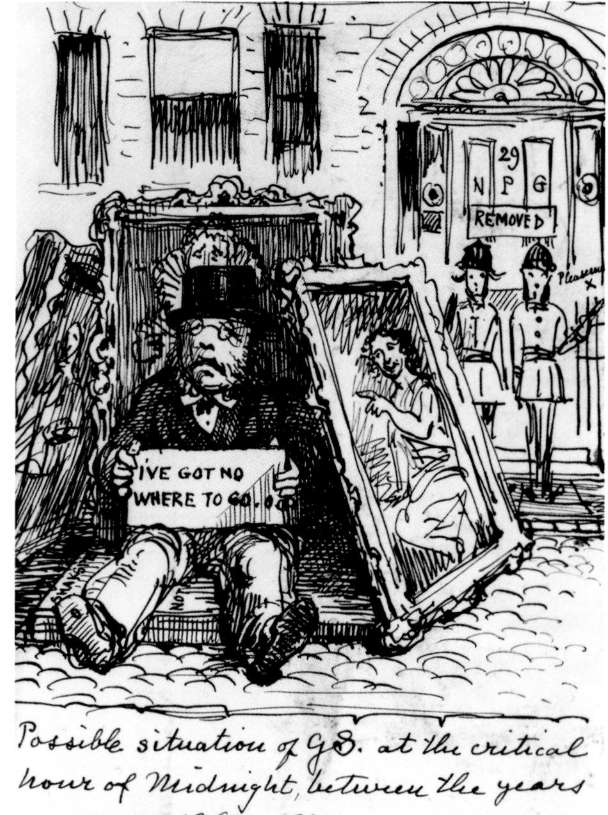

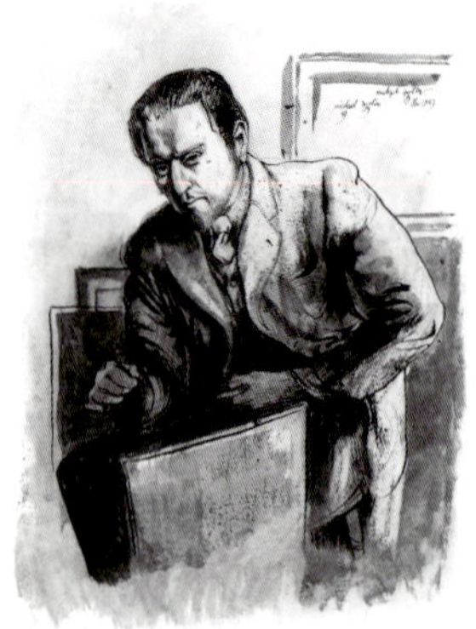

Michael Ayrton
(1921–75), 1947

Ayrton trained in Paris with
Giorgio de Chirico and Pavel
Tchelitchew. From 1944 he was
the art critic of the *Spectator*,
and in 1946 he worked with
Constant Lambert on Purcell's
Fairy Queen. Made ten years
earlier than the painting
opposite, Ayrton sports the same
beard and is conventionally
dressed. The desire to place the
figure within a space bounded
by juxtaposed straight lines is
already apparent.

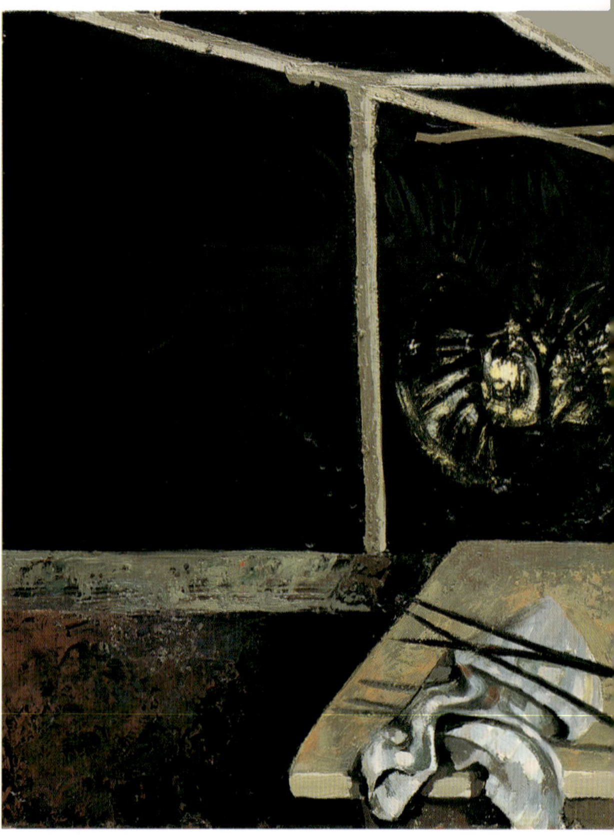

Michael Ayrton
1957–8

The linear scaffolding above Ayrton's head and the use of the device
of a mirror standing on a table to reflect his image create a feeling of
being out-of-body and project existential space. They also relate to
the constructivist geometry of John Tunnard's self-portrait (page 79)
and recall the cage-like structures used by Francis Bacon.

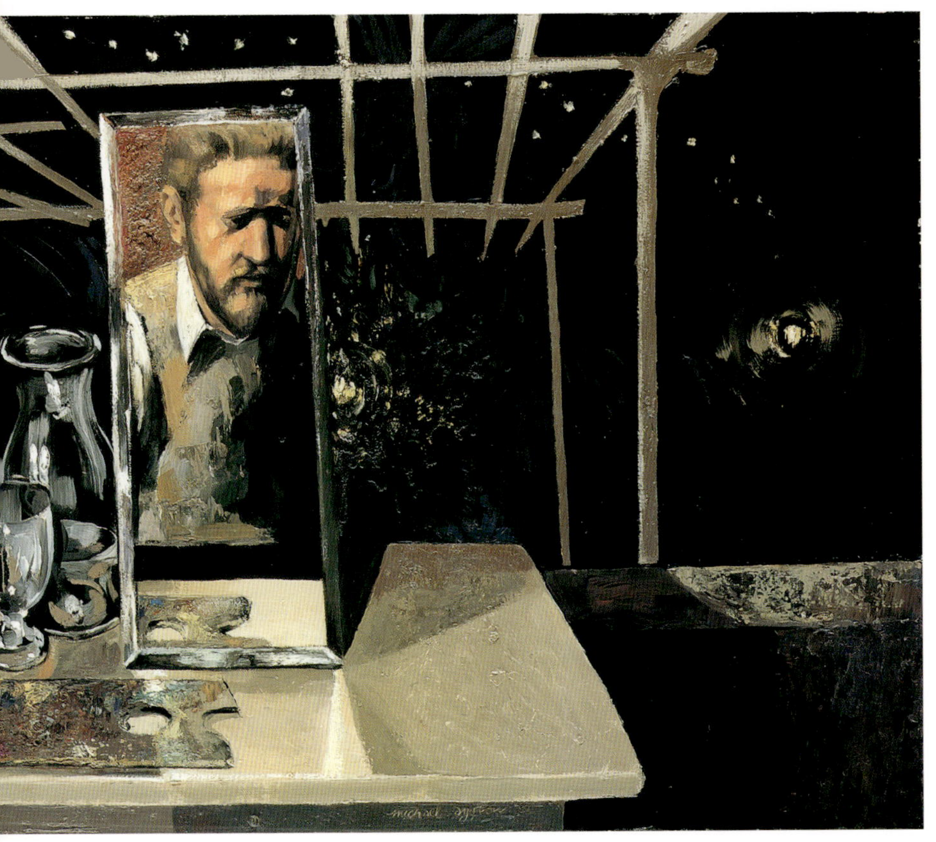

Self-portraits

Richard Hamilton
(b.1922), 1970

Hamilton was friend and collaborator of the conceptual artist Marcel
Duchamp and was strongly influenced by him. This self-portrait is
derived from a photograph taken by Francis Bacon in 1969, and
reproduced in Hamilton's book *Polaroid Portraits*, published in 1972,
where it occurs with a red background and in landscape format.
Always enthusiastically exploiting new media, including digital
technology, Hamilton in his screenprint makes a succinct comment on
the physical and psychological distortion found in Bacon's paintings.

Opposite:
Henryk Gotlib
(1890–1966), *c*.1942

Born in Cracow, Gotlib came to England in 1939, where he joined the
London Group. He considered himself a painter and used his plaster
self-portrait as the subject for a painting, transforming it into an alter-
ego and reinterpreting its form in another medium. Here the physical,
solid presence of the sculpture masquerades as an abstract self. His
use of paint on the highly absorbent plaster seems to emphasise his
physical involvement in the work.

Portraying the psyche

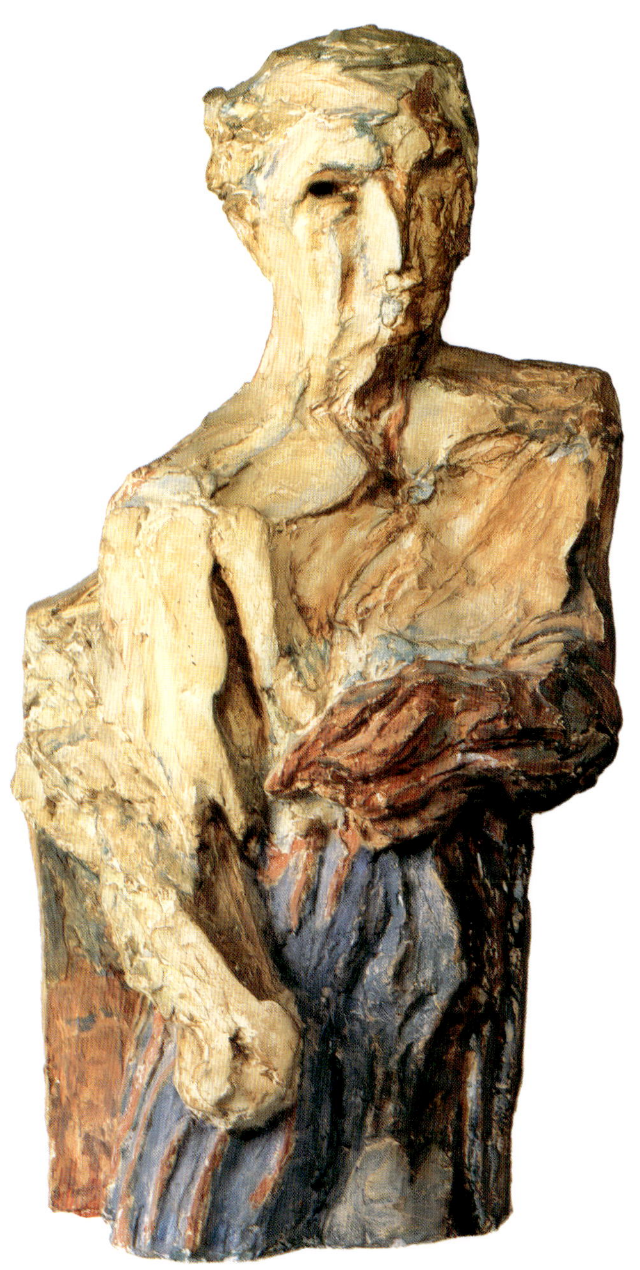

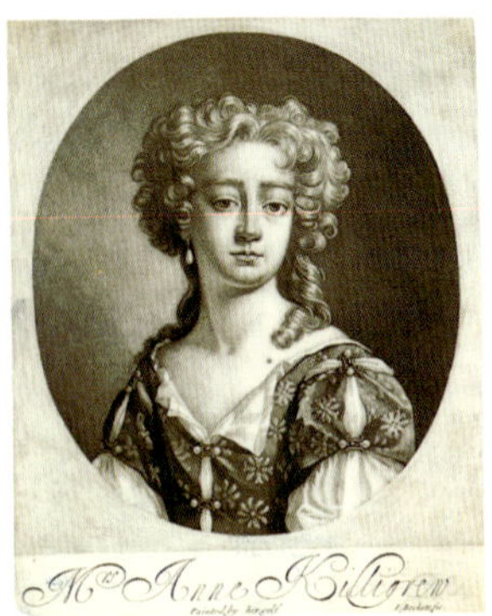

Anne Killigrew
(1660–85), published
c.1683–1729

In Restoration London, even
with wealth, education and
connections, it would have
been an achievement both to
compose poetry and paint
pictures. Anne Killigrew was
obviously precocious and
confident, as making a self-
portrait is a conscious gesture
of potential public self-exposure
that was unusual for a woman
at that time. She died aged
twenty-five, leaving in her desire
for recognition a short verse for
her epitaph: 'When I am Dead,
few Friends attend my Hearse,
/And for a Monument, I leave
my verse'.

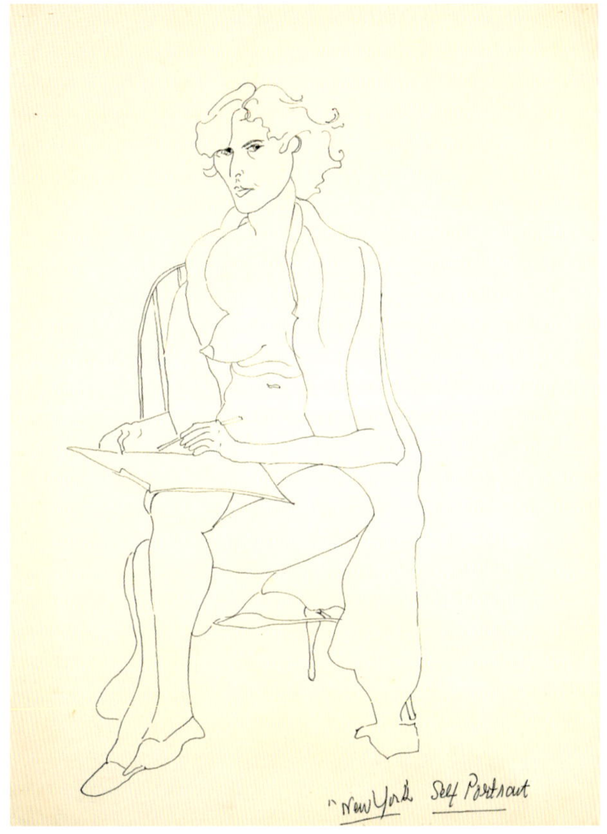

Oriel Ross
(1907–94), *c*.1928–31

Multi-talented, Ross trained at the Royal College of Music and made
her debut as an actor in 1923 aged sixteen. In 1928 she appeared as
Nature in Diaghilev's *Ballet Ode*, and then went to New York to work
in revue and cabaret on Broadway. As one of Ross's many methods
of self-expression, this drawing seems beautiful, lucid and effortless,
the fluid ink-line seamlessly transmitting the languorous essence of
the artist. This might also illustrate the meditative space the actor
needs in order to concentrate before or after a performance.

Portraying the psyche

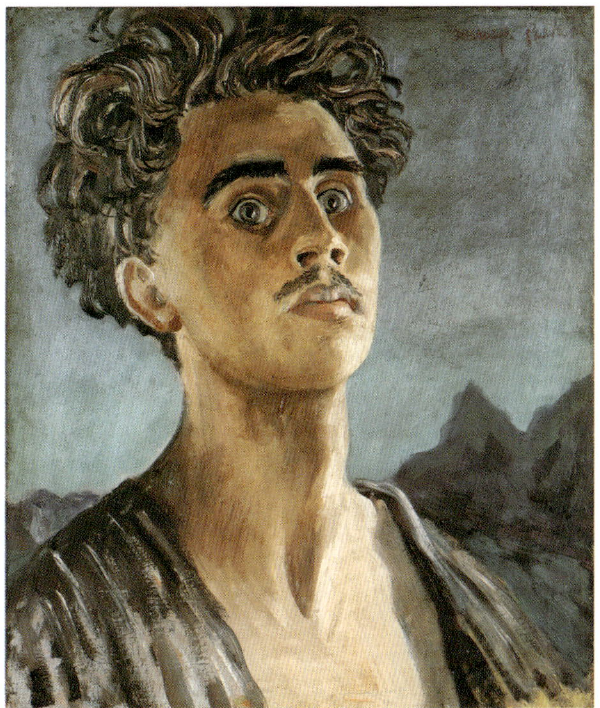

Mervyn Peake
(1911–61), 1932

The wide, sky-blue eyes, black eyebrows and disarrayed hair of the sitter give this self-portrait a charged and unsettling atmosphere. The 'peaks' in the background are an obvious and charming evocation of the artist's name. Peake considered himself a painter, but is best known for his original illustrations and writing, including poems, plays and nonsense verse, such as *The Trouble with Geraniums*:

> The trouble with myself is all self-centred in the eye
> The trouble with my looking glass, is that it shows me, me;
> There's trouble with all sorts of things where it should never be.

This self-portrait is wild and yet recognisably human, like the strange characters that inhabit his books, *Titus Groan* (1946), *Gormenghast* (1950), where the symbolism of the castle has been likened to the 'labyrinthine mind' and *Titus Alone* (1959).

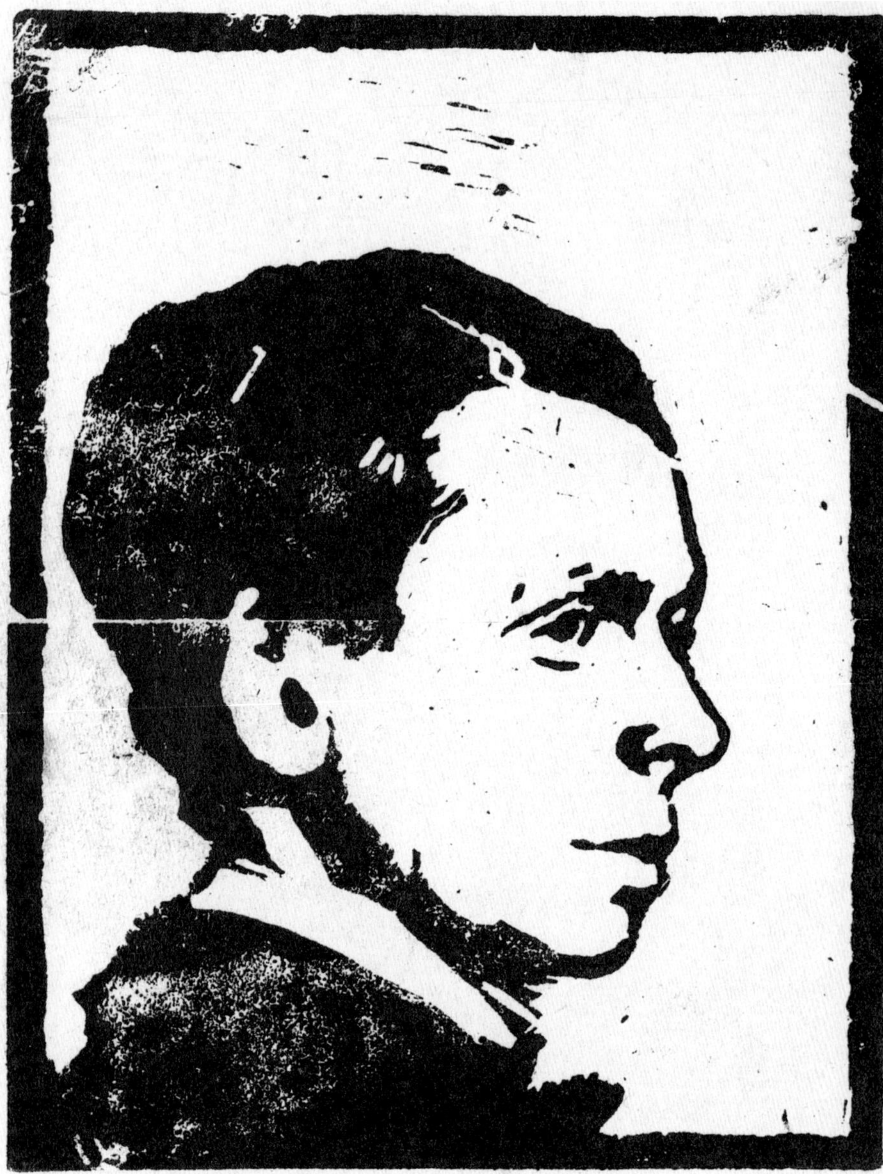

Chapter eight
A question of identity

All self-portraits are identity statements; the artists' own personal marks are an analogy between themselves and their work. The self-portrait can be a journey into the unknown, but artists like David Bomberg (page 96) who produced them throughout their lives often show an unmistakably identifiable thread running through from their first to their last self-portrait. Elements of personal style make up the constant, recognisable features recurring and characterising their work: as Julian Trevelyan (page 21) stated, 'The fact of what one paints and what one is is inescapably interwoven'. E.H. Gombrich describes the artist's need to possess a vocabulary before embarking on a 'copy' of reality. Being at ease and in control of the medium tends to be the prerogative of the mature artist.

In 1500 the young Albrecht Dürer painted a self-portrait which he described in his own words as being *'noch Christo z'leben'* – in the likeness of Jesus Christ. This might seem blasphemous, but Erwin Panofsky explains it as a way of showing the artist's mystical identification with God, from whom his creative genius as an artist is derived. This is reinforced by the frontal pose and the religious gesture of raised right hand, simultaneously evoking blessing and artistic virtuosity.

Disciplines such as miniature painting and ceramics may seem to focus the viewer's attention by technical brilliance in an unusual medium. Richard Cosway's touch at the end of the eighteenth century was dashing and brilliant – he is every inch the dandy – while Isaac Oliver's work two centuries earlier seems considered, more serious and meticulous (page 92). In the twentieth century, designer Susie Cooper is knowing, professional and witty (page 91). Focusing on what the work actually looks like, we need to attempt to define whether what we see is more than technical

Sir William Nicholson
(1872–1949), based on a photograph of 1912

From 1894 to 1895 Nicholson worked with his brother-in-law, James Pryde, as the print partnership J. & W. Beggarstaff. After this business collapsed he continued to work in the print medium for the publisher William Heinemann. This is one of two woodcut self-portraits; the other, *A was an Artist*, is from *Alphabet* (1898). Always a dandy, Nicholson based this print on an elegant portrait by a society photographer.

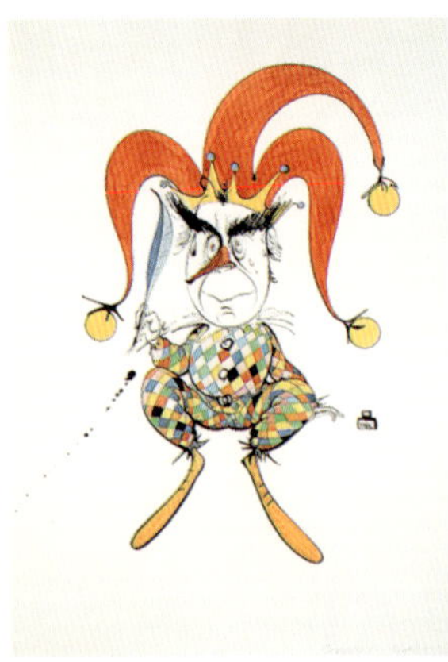

Gerald Scarfe
(b.1936), 1988

Scarfe here caricatures his own profession by depicting himself in a classic harlequin outfit, as a jester. The implication is that he exists outside social norms, not governed by the rules of the game. He gives himself the same harsh treatment as he gives the public figures whom he lampoons in his caricatures.

prowess. Could the energy associated with the differing styles of these artists be a reflection of their inner selves? Certainly the self-portrait is a highly personal, aesthetic investigation, whether or not it is made for public consumption.

Such a romantic concept of an imaginative journey in self-portraiture can seem obscure when applied to the discipline of painting. As Lucian Freud comments, 'I think, half the point of painting a picture is that you don't know what will happen … that if painters did know what was going to happen they wouldn't bother actually to do it' (interview by Martin Gayford, *Independent on Sunday*, 26 May 2002). This statement seems to encapsulate the nineteenth-century notion of the artist so aptly envisioned by James Sant (see page 22). Thomas Gainsborough was the great precursor of this bohemian attitude. He straddled the artistic time frame, catering for society's demands for portraits while simultaneously generating powerful personal works of his own. 'I wish you would recollect,' he said to a patron, 'that Painting and Punctuality mix like oil and vinegar, and that Genius and regularity are utter Enemies'. The energy of Gainsborough's personality erupts through his statements, yet his portrait aged thirty-one suggests a restrained and quiet personality. We cannot presume that technique is necessarily an indication of character, but this is an inevitable reaction when we view portraits – and even more so when they are self-portraits.

A question of identity

Susie Cooper (1902–95)
*c.*1933

This pouting face with carefully made up red lips has a certain Hollywood aura. Cooper's red, bow-shaped lips emphasise the mask-like quality of her self-portrait, using the shininess of the glaze to great effect. The simplified modelling proclaims her precise control and knowledge of the medium; her lustre curls in glaze eloquently suggesting real life. A ceramicist and successful businesswoman, known for her company's popular art-deco designs, Cooper was recognised for improving standards of lithographic transfer decoration.

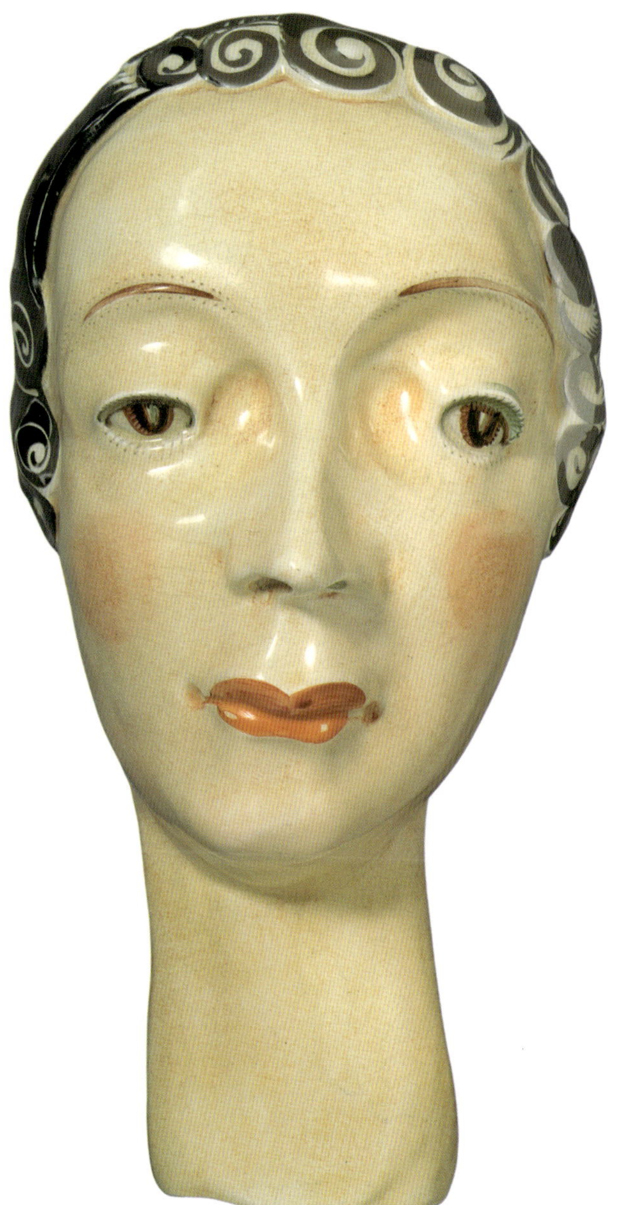

Self-portraits

Isaac Oliver
(*c*.1565–1617), *c*.1590

Oliver, a Huguenot refugee from Rouen, arrived in Britain in 1568. Made twenty-two years later, his self-portrait is elegant and has an unforced realism, which contrasts tellingly with the decorative sparkle of the work of his illustrious British predecessor Nicholas Hilliard. Thanks to Oliver's predilection for rendering form and character succinctly, in *c*.1592 he painted the only portrait in existence of Elizabeth I in which she looks her age.

Richard Cosway
(1742–1821), *c*.1790

Cosway collected old master drawings, dealt in pictures, was elected to the Royal Academy of Arts in 1771 and in 1785 became Principal Painter to the Prince of Wales (later George IV), to whose circle of friends he already belonged. In 1781 he married fellow miniaturist and teacher Maria Hadfield, Angelica Kauffmann's friend from Italy. The couple lived at Schomberg House, Pall Mall, from 1784, where Gainsborough was also resident. Cosway's 'Macaroni' tendencies (see page 31) are seen to good effect in this subtle portrait. The quality of delicate transparency that he achieves in watercolour, imbues the work with an exquisite atmosphere.

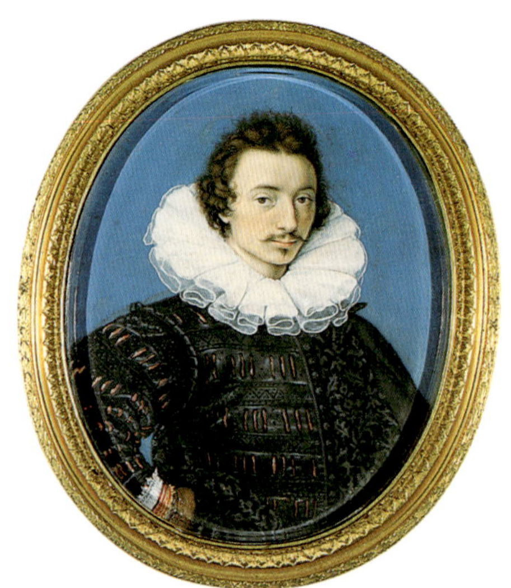

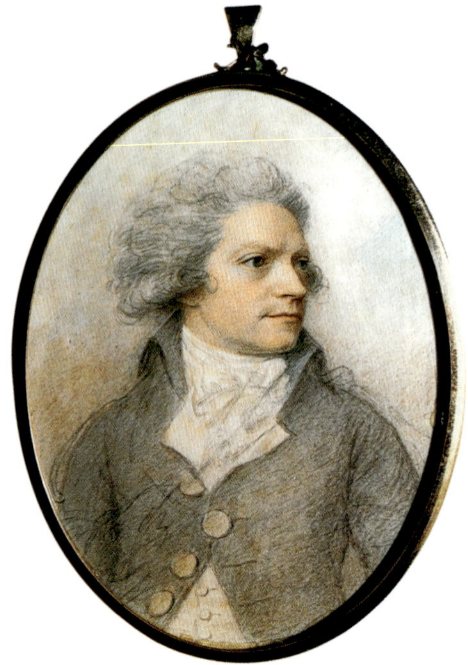

A question of identity

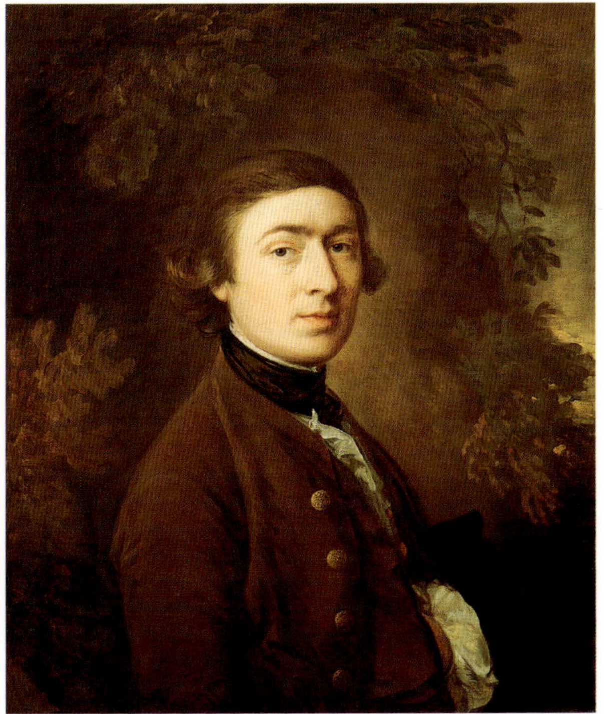

Thomas Gainsborough
(1727–88), *c.*1758–9

David Piper describes Gainsborough's late work as being 'almost airborne'; this extraordinary self-portrait seems to hover between the three periods of his artistic development. The work embodies the innocence of his Suffolk period (from 1748), the modelling apparent in his Bath period (from 1759) and a landscape backdrop, loose and free, that prefigures his late London style (from 1774). Gainsborough was known to set up still-life groupings of real twigs and branches in his studio from which to work. The background to this painting is unmistakably Gainsborough, revealing his passion for nature.

Self-portraits

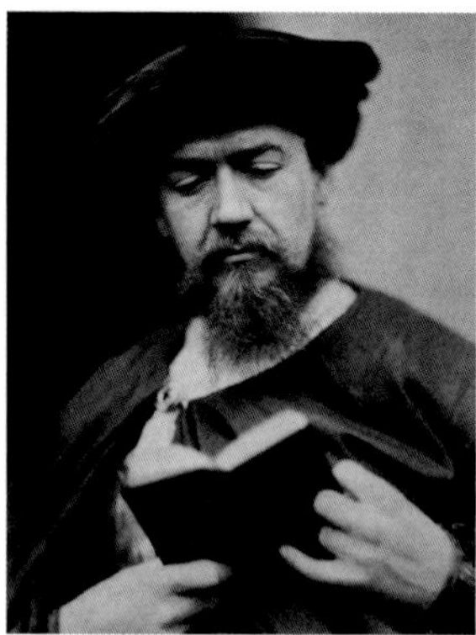

David Wilkie Wynfield
(1837–87), 1860s

Wynfield's namesake was his great uncle, godfather and renowned artist Sir David Wilkie (1785–1841). Wynfield was a member of the St John's Wood Clique, a group of artists whose works evoked another age (a good example is *And When Did You Last See Your Father?*, 1878, by William Yeames). Wynfield's attachment with the past manifested itself in works such as *The Death of Buckingham* (exhibited at the Royal Academy in 1871), which portrayed the murdered favourite of Charles I. This sensitive, demure and rather reticent image is one of a remarkable series of costume portraits that he made. Wynfield died of tuberculosis aged fifty and is buried in Highgate Cemetery.

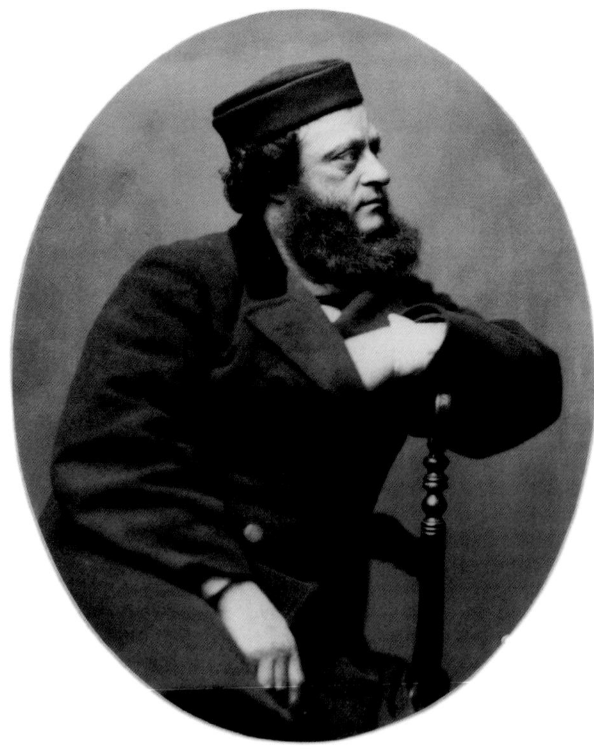

Oliver François Xavier Sarony
(1820–79), late 1850s

Born in Quebec, Sarony trained as a daguerreotypist in New York before travelling to Ireland and then England, where he set up his studio. A talented salesman, he encouraged his clients to buy hand-coloured enlargements of their portraits at 150 guineas apiece. Here his well-tailored coat and cap suggest the successful businessman rather than the working craftsman.

Opposite:
John Constable
(1776–1837), *c*.1799–1804

This self-portrait reflects a modest yet perfect gentleman. It gives little idea either of Constable's technical genius, nor of his remarkable observations of changing cloud formations and commitment to the *plein air* study of '… old rotten planks, slimy posts and brickwork, I love such things … Painting is but another word for feeling'.

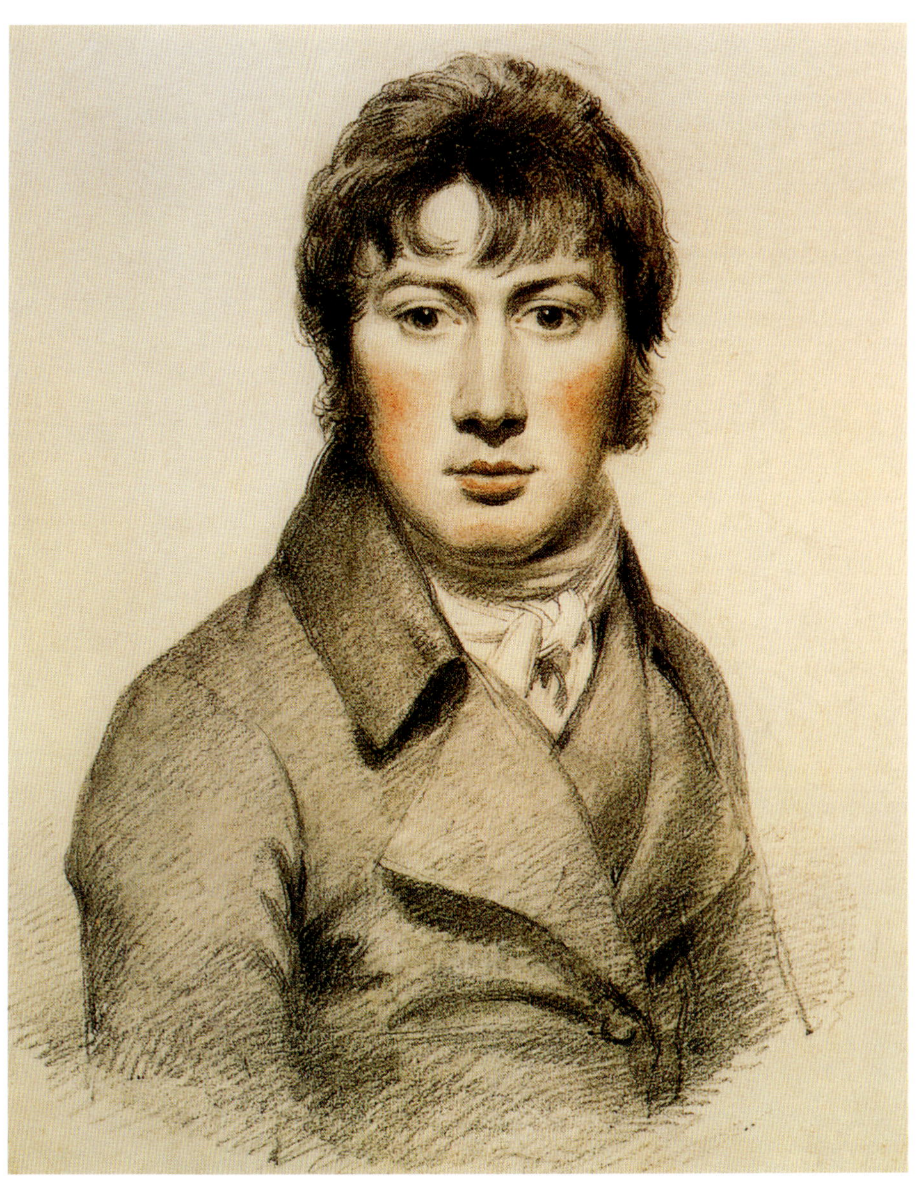

Self-portraits

David Bomberg
(1890–1957), 1937

Using an eraser to enhance the chiaroscuro of this black charcoal, Bomberg depicts himself fixing the viewer with a disdainful gaze as he smokes his cigarette. The signature is energetic, spiky, concise; a bravura finale to an explosive drawing. Between 1945 and 1953 Bomberg taught at Borough Polytechnic, where Frank Auerbach (b.1931) and Leon Kossoff (b.1922) were his students. Kossoff remembers watching Bomberg at work: 'Once I watched him draw over a student's drawing. I saw the flow of form. I saw the likeness to the sitter appear. It seemed an encounter with what was already there and I'll never forget it.'

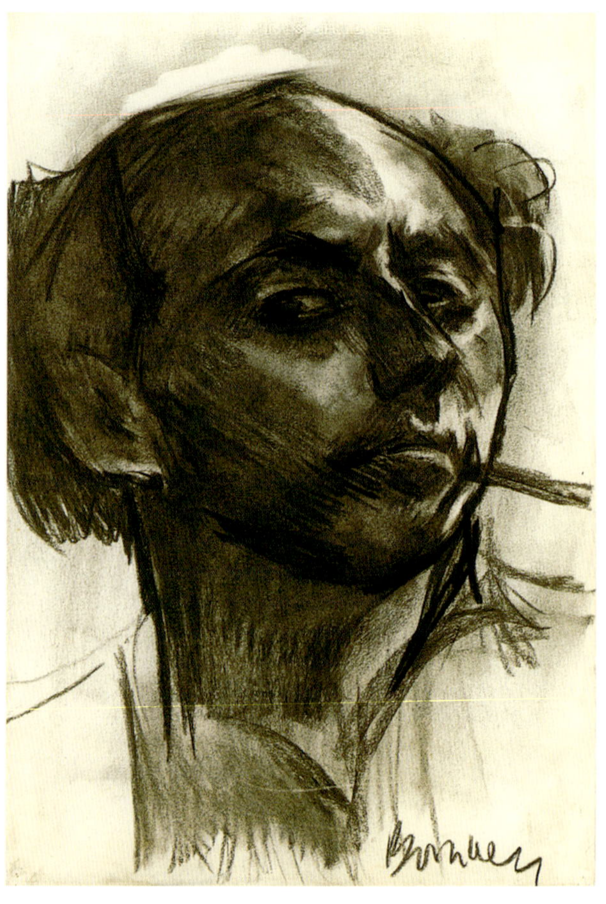

Opposite:
Frank Auerbach
(b.1931), 1994–2001

David Bomberg taught Auerbach passion for 'form' and Auerbach remarked that 'It was those standards and his [Bomberg's] impatience with anything less that I found stimulating'. Auerbach is known for this same passion and for the amount of time he spends reworking the subjects of his works, as revealed by the dating of this drawing.

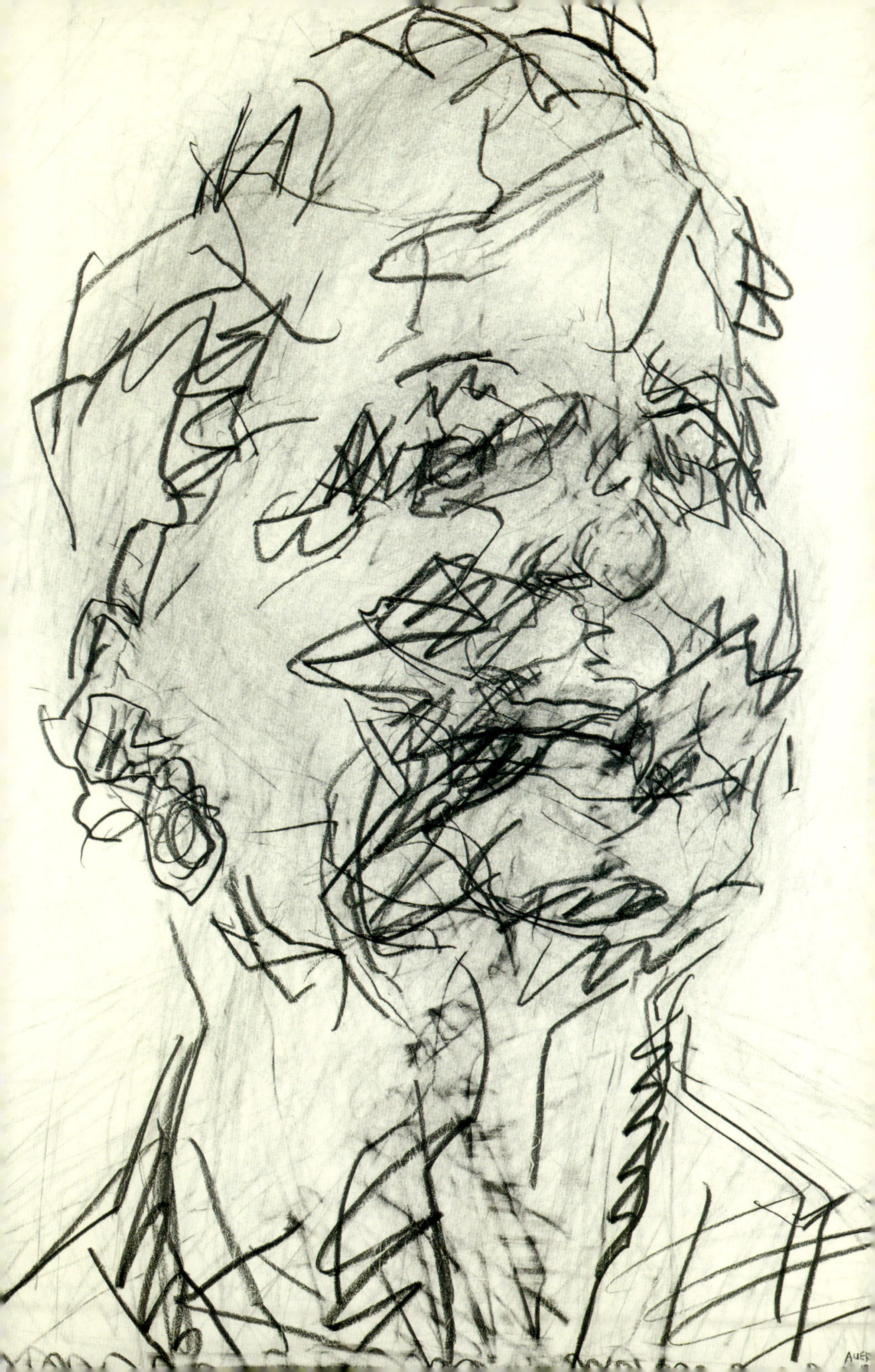

Self-portraits

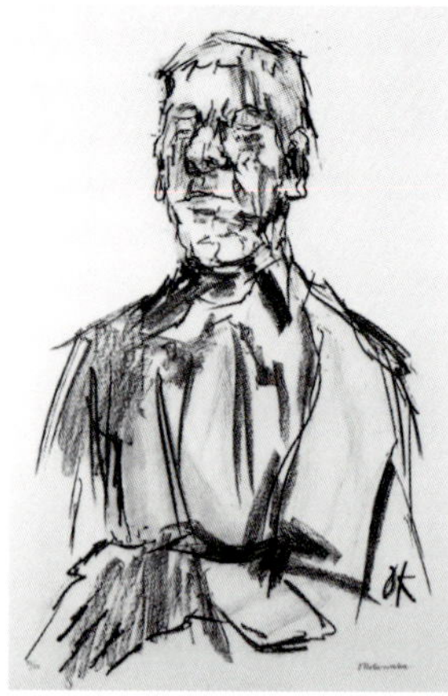

Oskar Kokoschka
(1886–1980), 1965

Kokoschka had been one of the most prominent artists represented in the Nazi Entartete Kunst (Degenerate Art) Exhibition, which opened on 19 July 1937. Despite the fact that the lithograph was not made until 1965, almost thirty years later, it still pulses with all the energy of his early Expressionist period. Kokoschka's signature style is reflected in the fluid energy of his vibrant line. He produced many self-portraits, often using himself as the model for his allegorical works. This lithograph was used as the poster image for his eightieth birthday exhibition in Leiden.

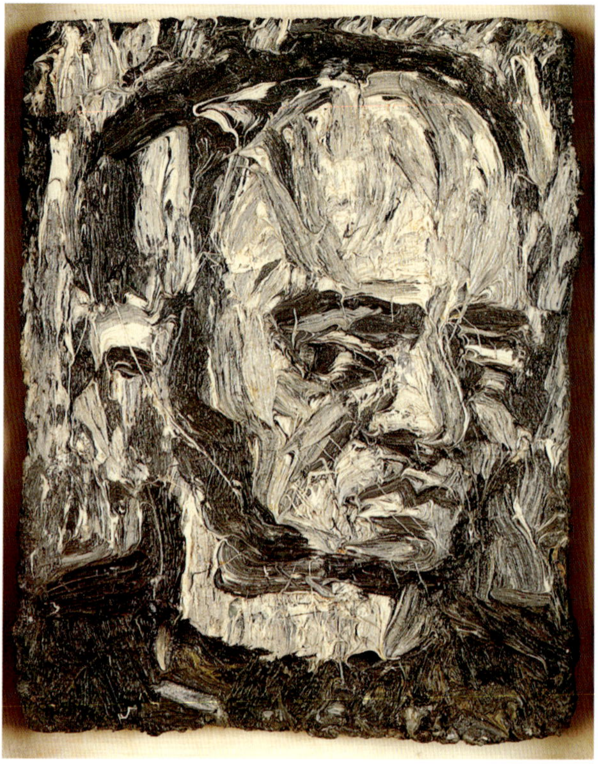

Leon Kossoff
(b.1922), 1981

The physicality of paint, built up and moved about on the surface, gives this portrait a palpable presence. The monotone pattern of black and white is stark and uncompromising, suggesting that this is as much a statement about three-dimensional paint style than a matter of producing a recognisable self-portrait. Kossoff's distinctive style, however, is instantly identifiable.

Opposite:
Barbara Hepworth (1903–75), 1950

Barbara Hepworth's elegant but intense self-portrait belongs to a small group of figurative works from the late 1940s to the early 1950s. Like the preceding group of Expressionist self-portraits, she also sees herself in terms of her own, albeit very different, graphic style, literally incising her pencil into the pre-prepared gesso board.

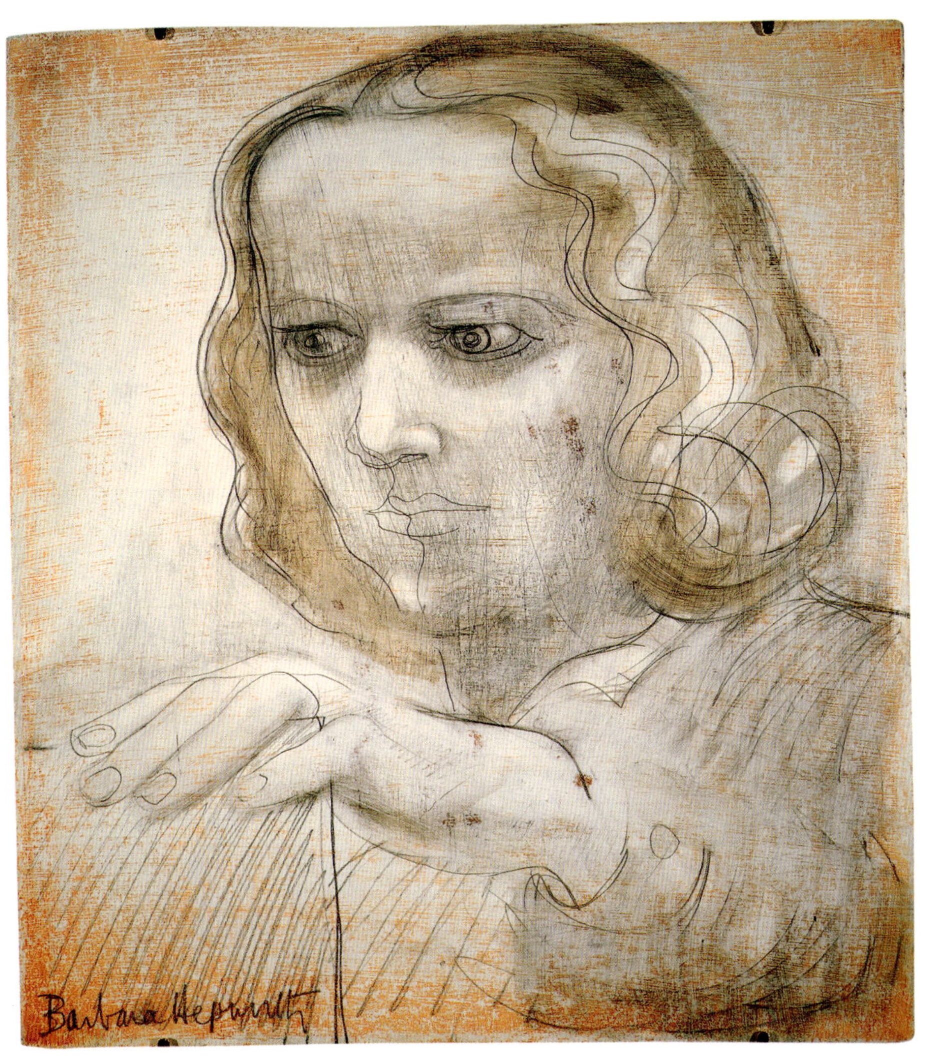
Barbara Hepworth

Self-portraits

Lucian Freud
(b.1922), 1963

Sigmund Freud's grandson
Lucian was born in Berlin,
arriving in England in 1933. He
studied for a period in Suffolk
with Cedric Morris (see page 59).
This self-portrait, made over
forty years ago, is intense and
unflinching. The brush and
paintwork is both smoother
and more stylised than today,
but his characteristic dun-
coloured palette is something
he retains. An arresting
confrontational study, this self-
portrait marks a distancing from
the minute attention to detail in
his major portraits of the 1950s.

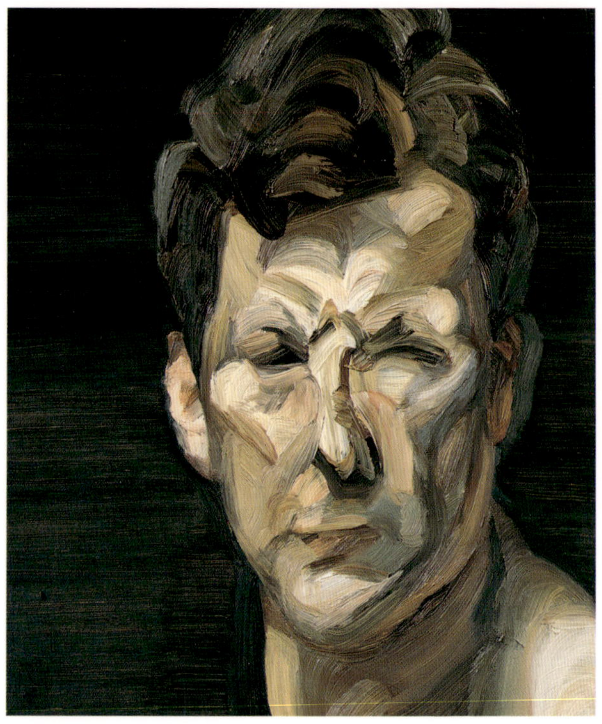

Opposite:
Gwen John
(1876–1939), *c.*1900

Using the whole body to fill a canvas is an effective way of suggesting
strength of character. Gwen John was fiercely independent, with
passions for art, people and religion. The strong composition of this
self-portrait acts as a visual counterpoint to the delicate, chalky paint
surface and muted palette. Meticulous in her colour selections and
technique, she consistently refined her process of paint application
over the years. John's work has been described as having a 'private
incandescence of spirit'. She studied at the Slade, and in Paris from
1898 to 1900, with Whistler, who famously declared that she had a
'fine sense of tone'. Living in France from 1903, she was Rodin's
muse and lover, and also friend to Rainer Maria Rilke, his biographer
and secretary.

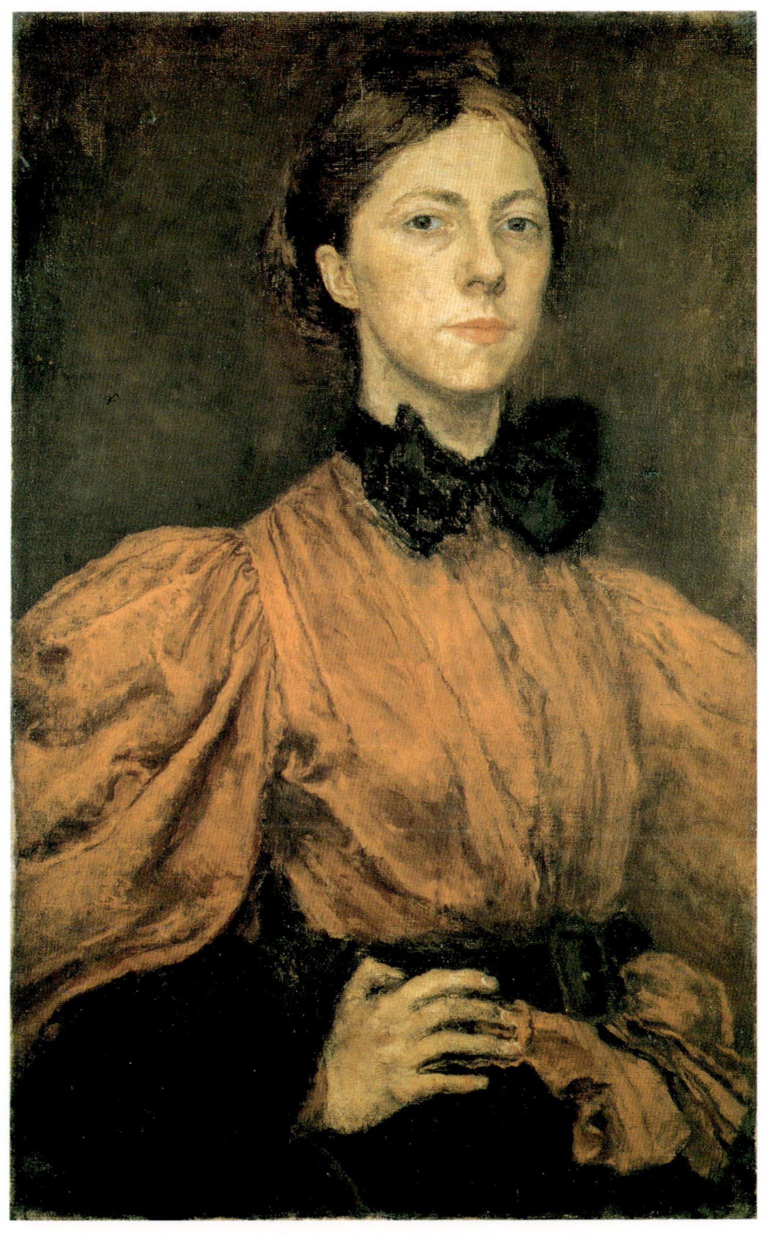

Select bibliography

Allen, Brian, *Francis Hayman* (Yale University Press, Newhaven, and London, 1987)

Ames-Lewis, Francis, *The Intellectual life of the Early Renaissance Artist* (Yale University Press, Newhaven, and London, 2000)

Andrews, Allen, *The Life of L.S. Lowry, A Biography* (Jupiter Books, London, 1977)

Bell, Julian, *Five Hundred Self-portraits* (Phaidon, London, 2000)

Brooke, Xanthe, *Face to Face: Three Centuries of Artists' Self-Portraiture* (exh. cat., Bluecoat Press for Walker Art Gallery, National Museums & Galleries on Merseyside, Liverpool, 1995)

Brunon, Bernard, *Autoportraits Contemporains: Here's Looking at Me* (Espace Lyonnais d'Art Contemporain, Ville de Lyon, France, 1993)

Campbell, Lorne, *Renaissance Portraits: European portrait painting in the 14th, 15th and 16th centuries* (Yale University Press, New Haven, and London, 1990)

Chadwick, Whitney (ed.), *Mirror Images, Women, Surrealism & Self-representation* (MIT Press, Cambridge, Massachusetts, and London, 1998)

Chenoune, Farid, *A History of Men's Fashion* (Flammarion, Paris, 1993)

Cork, Richard, *David Bomberg* (exh. cat., Tate, London, 1988)

Csikszentmihalyi, Mihaly, *Creativity: Flow and the psychology of discovery and invention* (HarperCollins, New York, 1996)

Delpire, Robert (ed.) *Identitiés: De Disderi au Photomaton* (Centre Nationale de la Photographie/Édition du Chêne, Paris, 1985)

Egerton, Judy, in *Van Dyck 1599–1641* (exh. cat., Royal Academy of Arts, London, and Antwerpen Open, 1999)

Eggum, Arne, in *Edvard Munch, Symbols & Images* (exh. cat., National Gallery of Art, Washington, 1978)

Fleming-Williams, Ian, Parris, Leslie, and Shields, Conal, *Constable: Paintings, Watercolours & Drawings* (exh. cat., Tate, London, 1976)

Fraser Jenkins, David, and Langdale, Cecily, *Gwen John: An Interior Life* (exh. cat., Phaidon, and Barbican Art Gallery, London, 1985

Gibson, Robin, *Glyn Philpot 1884–1937, Edwardian Aesthete to Thirties Modernist* (National Portrait Gallery, London, 1984)

Graham, Rigby, and Spalding, Frances, *John Minton: 1917–1957: A Selective Retrospective* (exh. cat., Oriel Davies Gallery, Newtown, Powys, Wales, 1994)

Hamilton, Richard (ed.), *Polaroid Portraits* (Mathews Miller Dunbar, London, 1972)

Hilliard, Nicholas, *A Treatise Concerning the Arte of Limning* (1598; Carcanet New Press, Ashington, 1981)

Hockney, David, *That's the way I see it*, ed. Nikos Stangos (Thames and Hudson, London, 1993)

Hogarth, William, *The Analysis of Beauty* (printed for the author by J. Reeves, London, 1753)

Hopkins, Justine, *Michael Ayrton: A Biography* (Andre Deutsch, London, 1994)

Irmas, Deborah, and Sobieszek, Robert, *The Camera i: Photographic Self-portraits from the Audrey and Sydney Irmas Collection* (Los Angeles County Museum of Art, Harry N. Abrams, New York, 1994)

Josipovici, Gabriel, *Touch: an essay* (Yale University Press, New Haven, and London, 1996)

Kemp, Martin, ''*Ogni dipintore dipinge se*': A Neoplatonic Echo in Leonardo's Art Theory?' In *Cultural Aspects of the Italian Renaissance*, ed. Cecil Clough (Manchester University Press, Manchester, 1976)

Kimmelman, Michael, *Portraits: Talking with Artists at The Met, The Modern, The Louvre and Elsewhere* (Random House, New York, 1999)

Kinneir, Joan (ed.), Introduction by David Piper, *The Artist by Himself: Self-Portraits from Youth to Old Age* (Paul Elek, London, 1980)

Lévêque, Jean-Jacques, *Henri Fantin-Latour* (ACR Editions, Paris, 1996)

Lingwood, James (ed.), *Staging the Self: Self-Portrait Photography 1840s–1980s* (National Portrait Gallery, London, 1986)

Morphet, Richard, *Cedric Morris* (exh. cat., Tate, London, 1984)

Ormond, Richard, *Artists at Work* (National Portrait Gallery, London, 1981)

Parry, Graham, *The Golden Age Restor'd: The Culture of the Stuart Court, 1603–42. The Court of Charles I* (Manchester University Press, Manchester, and Dover, New Hampshire, 1989)

Piper, David, *The English Face* (National Portrait Gallery, London, 1978)

Peat, Alan, and Whitton, Brian A., *John Tunnard: his life & work* (Scolar Press, Hants, England, and Vermont, USA, 1997)

Richardson, Jonathan, *An Essay on the Theory of Painting* (1715; Scolar Press, Hants, 1971)

Rideal, Liz, *Mirror Mirror: Self-Portraits by Women Artists* (National Portrait Gallery, London, 2001)

Rychlik, Otmar, *Arnulf Rainer, Alte Meister* (exh. cat., Galerie Krinzinger, Innsbruck, Austria, 1989)

Scharf, Aaron, *Art and Photography* (Penguin, London, 1968)

Stoichita, Victor I., *A Short History of the Shadow* (Reaktion Books Ltd, London, 1997)

Trevelyan, Julian, *Indigo Days: The Art and Memoirs of Julian Trevelyan (1957;* Scolar Press, Hants, England, and Vermont, USA, 1996)

Varnedoe, J. Kirk T., *Modern Portraits, The Self & Others* (Columbia University, New York, 1976)

Wark, R.R., 'A note on Van Dyck's Self-Portrait with Sunflower' (*Burlington Magazine*, XCVIII, 1956)

List of illustrations

Unless otherwise stated all images are © National Portrait Gallery, London

Title page and introduction
p.4 **L.S. (Laurence Stephen) Lowry**, self-portrait, 1938. Oil on canvas, 535 x 435mm (21 x 17⅛").
© Rothschild Trust Company Inc/National Portrait Gallery, London NPG L224; p.6 **Angelica Kauffmann**,
self-portrait, c.1770–75. Oil on canvas, 737 x 610mm (29 x 24"). NPG 430; p.8 (above) **View of the 18th
Century Galleries** and (below) **view of the 20th Century Galleries at the National Portrait Gallery,
London**. Photographs © Liz Rideal; p.9 **Sir Joshua Reynolds**, self-portrait, c.1747–9. Oil on canvas,
635 x 743mm (25 x 29¼"). NPG 41; p.10 (detail) *Identity*, Liz Rideal, 1985. Photographic collage,
2000 x 5000mm (79 x 197"). © Liz Rideal/National Portrait Gallery, London NPG D11008; p.11 **Dame
Ethel Walker**, self-portrait, c.1925. Oil on canvas, 613 x 508mm (24⅛ x 20"). NPG 5301.

Chapter one
p.12 **George Frederic Watts**, self-portrait, c.1879. Oil on canvas, 635 x 508mm (25 x 20"). NPG 1406;
p.14 *Self-portrait with Skull*, Sarah Lucas, 1997. Iris print, 737 x 482mm (29 x 19"). © Sarah Lucas.
NPG P884(8); p.15 **Edward Collier**, self-portrait, 1683. Oil on canvas, 444 x 528mm (17½ x 20¾").
NPG 6069; p.16 **John Minton**, self-portrait, c.1953. Oil on canvas, 356 x 254mm (14 x 10"). © Royal
College of Art. NPG 4620; p.17 *Vanitas II*, Helen Chadwick, 1986. Cibachrome print, 509 x 510mm
(20 x 20"). © Helen Chadwick Estate. Courtesy Zelda Cheatle Gallery. NPG P874; p.18 **John Bratby**, self-
portrait, 1967. Oil on canvas, 1676 x 914mm (66 x 36"). Collection © courtesy of the artist's estate/www.
bridgeman.co.uk. NPG 6555; p.19 **Dame Laura Knight**, self-portrait, 1913. Oil on canvas, 1524 x 1276mm
(60 x 50¼"). © The Estate of Dame Laura Knight 2005. All Rights Reserved, DACS. NPG 4839; p.20
Thomas Kerrich, self-portrait, 1774. Chalk, 433 x 300mm (17 x 11¾"). NPG 6531; p.21 **Julian Otto
Trevelyan**, self-portrait, 1940. Oil on canvas, 611 x 464mm (24 x 18¼"). NPG 5807.

Chapter two
p.22 **James Sant**, self-portrait, c.1840. Oil on canvas, 591 x 441mm (23¼ x 17⅜"). NPG 4093; p.25 **Sir
William Orpen**, self-portrait, 1910. Pencil and wash, diameter 330mm (13"). NPG 2638; p.26 **Sir Roger
de Grey**, self-portrait, 1990. Oil on canvas, 1270 x 1012mm (50 x 39⅞"). NPG 6246; p.27 **George Arnald**,
self-portrait, 1831. Oil on canvas, 749 x 622mm (29½ x 24½"). NPG 5254; p.28 (above) **Bill Brandt**, self-
portrait, 1966. Bromide print, 342 x 291mm (13½ x 11½"). © Bill Brandt Archive. NPG x22409; (below)
Harry Borden, self-portrait, 1998. C-print, 225 x 205mm (8⅞ x 8⅛"). © Harry Borden. NPG x87889; p.29
(above) *Malice through the looking glass*, Mike McCartney with Roberta (Bobby) Brown, Mike
McCartney, 1962. Bromide print, 255 x 255mm (10 x 10"). © Michael McCartney. NPG x88784; (below)
Pamela Chandler with Mary Morris, Pamela Chandler, 1963. Modern print from an original negative,
341 x 267mm (13⅜ x 10½"). © Estate of Pamela Chandler/National Portrait Gallery, London NPG x88817.

Chapter three
p.30 **Philippe Jacques de Loutherbourg**, self-portrait, c.1805–10. Oil on canvas, 1270 x 1016mm
(50 x 40"). NPG 2493; p.32 **Francis Frith**, self-portrait, 1857. Albumen print, 186 x 142mm (7⅜ x 5⅝").
NPG x13682; p.33 **Brian Griffin**, self-portrait, 1988. Bromide print, 354 x 357mm (13⅞ x 14"). © Brian
Griffin. NPG x125281; p.34 (left) **Richard Cockle Lucas**, self-portrait, c.1858. Albumen carte-de-visite,
86 x 42mm (3⅜ x 1⅝"). NPG Ax23435; (right) self-portrait, c.1858. Albumen carte-de-visite, 94 x 61mm
(3⅜ x 2⅜"). NPG Ax23434; p.35 *The Last Thing I said to you is don't leave me here. 1*, Tracey Emin,
2000. Epson print, 813 x 1092mm (32 x 43"). © Tracey Emin. NPG P879; p.36 **Cecil Beaton**, self-portrait,
1933. Bromide print, 217 x 173mm (8½ x 6¾"). © By courtesy of Cecil Beaton Studio Archive, Sotheby's.
NPG x40424; p.37 *Self Portrait in a Single Breasted Suit with Hare*, Sam Taylor-Wood, 2001. C-print,
1521 x 1046mm (59⅞ x 41⅛"). © Sam Taylor-Wood. NPG P959; p.38 **Wyndham Lewis**, self-portrait, 1932.

Ink and wash, 254 x 197mm (10 x 7¾"). © Wyndham Lewis and the estate of the late Mrs G.A. Lewis by kind permission of the Wyndham Lewis Memorial Trust (a registered charity). NPG 4528; p.39 **Lee Miller**, self-portrait, 1943. Modern print from an original negative, 254 x 204mm (10 x 8"). © Lee Milller Archives. All rights reserved 2005. NPG P1082; p.40 **Harold Knight**, self-portrait, c.1923. Oil on canvas, 914 x 711mm (36 x 28"). © The Estate of Harold Knight 2005. All Rights Reserved, DACS. NPG 4831; p.41 **Doris Zinkeisen**, self-portrait, exhibited 1929. Oil on canvas, 1072 x 866mm (42¼ x 34⅛"). © Estate of Doris Clare Zinkeisen/National Portrait Gallery, London NPG 6487.

Chapter four
p.42 **Lewis Morley** with Patricia Morley, Lewis Morley, 1959. Bromide print, 381 x 290mm (15 x 11⅜"). © Lewis Morley, Lewis Morley Archive/Akehurst Creative Management. NPG x38901; p.44 (above) **David Octavius Hill**, Hill & Adamson, c.1843. Calotype, 197 x 137mm (7¾ x 5⅜"). NPG P6(1); (below) **Robert Adamson**, Hill & Adamson, 1843–8. Calotype, 201 x 144mm (7⅞ x 5⅝"). NPG P6(181); p.45 *In the Piss*, Gilbert & George, 1997. Photo piece of nine panels, 2260 x 1900mm (89 x 74¾"). © Gilbert & George. NPG 6489; p.46 **Gerlach Flicke** and Henry Strangwish, Gerlach Flicke, 1554. Oil on paper or vellum laid on panel, 88 x 119mm (3½ x 4¾"). NPG 6353; p.47 **Francis Hayman** and Grosvenor Bedford, Francis Hayman, c.1748–50. Oil on canvas, 718 x 914mm (28¼ x 36"). NPG 217; p.48 *A Conversation of Virtuosis … at the Kings Arms (A Club of Artists)*, Gawen Hamilton,1735. Oil on canvas, 876 x 1115mm (34½ x 43⅞"). NPG 1384; p.49 **Margaret MacGregor 'Peggy' Angus**, with James Ramsay MacDonald and members of his family, Peggy Angus, 1930s. Oil on plywood, 608 x 508mm (24 x 20"). © Estate of Peggy Angus/National Portrait Gallery, London NPG 6102; p.50 **William Roberts** and Sarah Roberts, William Roberts, 1975. Oil on canvas, 762 x 642mm (30 x 25¼"). Reproduced by permission of the William Roberts Society. NPG 5808; p.51 **Benjamin Brecknell Turner** with his wife Agnes Brecknell Turner, Benjamin Brecknell Turner, 1850s. Albumen print, 285 x 370mm (11¼ x 14½"). NPG P1003; p.52 **George Smith** and John Smith, George Smith, c.1760. Oil on canvas, 629 x 752mm (24¾ x 29⅝"). NPG 4117; p.53 **John Hamilton Mortimer** with a student, after a self-portrait of c.1765. Oil on canvas, 737 x 610mm (29 x 24"). NPG 234.

Chapter five
p.54 **Sir Godfrey Kneller**, self-portrait, c.1706–11 (detail). Oil on canvas, 464 x 356mm (18¼ x 14"). NPG 3214; p.56 **Sir Anthony van Dyck**, Wenceslaus Hollar, 1644, after Sir Anthony van Dyck's self-portrait of c.1633. Etching, 116 x 101mm (4⅝ x 4"). NPG D1326; p.57 *The Student – Homage to Picasso*, David Hockney, 1973. Etching, 572 x 435mm (22½ x 17⅝"). © David Hockney 1973. NPG 5280; p.58 **William Hogarth**, self-portrait, c.1757. Oil on canvas, 451 x 425mm (17¼ x 16¾"). NPG 289; p.59 (left) **X-ray of William Hogarth's self-portrait of c.1757**. NPG RN59485; (right) **Sir Cedric Lockwood Morris**, self-portrait, c.1930. Oil on canvas, 727 x 489mm (28⅝ x 19¼"). NPG 5407; p.60 (above) **Sir George Frampton**, self-portrait, 1894. Pencil, 490 x 386mm (19¼ x 15¼"). NPG 3043; pp.60 (below, detail) & 61 **James Abbott McNeill Whistler**, Percy Thomas after a self-portrait by James Abbott McNeill Whistler, 1874. Etching, 546 x 445mm (21½ x 17½"). NPG D4997; p.62 **Edward Lear**, self-portrait, 1864. Pen and ink, 140 x 175mm (5½ x 6⅞"). NPG 4351; p.63 **John Havinden**, self-portrait, 1930. Bromide print, 254 x 203mm (10 x 8"). © Estate of John Havinden. NPG P350; p.64 **Michael Dahl**, self-portrait, 1691. Oil on canvas, 1245 x 991mm (49 x 39"). NPG 3822; p.65 **Mary Beale**, self-portrait, c.1665. Oil on canvas, 1092 x 876mm (43 x 34½"). NPG 1687.

Chapter six
p.66 (clockwise from top left) **Jonathan Richardson**, self-portrait, 1729. Oil on canvas, 737 x 629mm (29 x 24¾"). NPG 706; self-portrait, 1735. Black chalk heightened with white on blue paper, 327 x 267mm (12⅞ x 10½"). NPG 3779; self-portrait, early 1730s. Black and red chalk, 397 x 257mm (15⅝ x 10⅛"). NPG 1693; self-portrait, 1736 (detail). Pen and pencil, 162 x 114mm (6⅜ x 4½"). NPG 3023; p.68 **Glyn Philpot**, self-portrait, 1908. Oil on canvas, 914 x 711mm (36 x 28"). © Estate of Glyn Philpot/National Portrait Gallery, London NPG 4681; p.69 (above) **Isaac Fuller**, self-portrait, c.1670. Oil on canvas,

1257 x 1003mm (49½ x 39½"). NPG 2104; (below) **Sir Peter Lely**, self-portrait, *c*.1660. Oil on canvas, 1080 x 876mm (42½ x 34½"). NPG 3897; p.70 **Walter Sickert**, self-portrait, 1930. Oil on canvas, 686 x 254mm (27 x 10"). © Estate of Walter Sickert; collection National Portrait Gallery, London NPG 3134; p.71 **Jo Spence**, self-portrait in collaboration with Dr Tim Sheard from the fifth triptych of *Triple Somersaults*, 1990. Colour print, 409 x 285mm (16⅛ x 11¼"). © Jo Spence Memorial Archive, London. NPG P849; p.72 **Dorothy Wilding**, self-portrait, 1920s. Chlorobromide print on tissue and card mount, 151 x 111mm (6 x 4⅜"). © Tom Hustler/National Portrait Gallery, London NPG x27401; p.73 **Dorothy Wilding**, self-portrait, 1956. Contact print, 139 x 118mm (5½ x 4⅝"). © Tom Hustler/National Portrait Gallery, London NPG x35930; p.74 (left) **Madame Yevonde**, self-portrait, 1967. Bromide print, 375 x 300mm (14¾ x 11¾"). © Yevonde Portrait Archive. NPG x17998; (right) self-portrait, 1925. Chlorobromide print on black paper mount, 198 x 242mm (7¾ x 9½"). © Yevonde Portrait Archive. NPG x11823; p.75 **Madame Yevonde**, self-portrait, 1970. Bromide print, 110 x 93mm (4⅜ x 3⅝"). © Yevonde Portrait Archive. NPG x33564.

Chapter seven

p.76 **Ithell Colquhoun**, self-portrait, 1930s. Ink and wash, 458 x 324mm (18 x 12¾"). NPG 6485; p.79 **John Tunnard**, self-portrait, 1959. Oil on board, 607 x 765mm (23⅞ x 30⅛"). NPG 6188; p.80 **Sir Francis Leggatt Chantrey**, self-portrait, *c*.1800. Pencil and grey wash, 136 x 143mm (5⅜ x 5⅝"). NPG 2103a; p.81 **Sir George Scharf**, self-portrait, 1869. Pen and ink, 178 x 111mm (7 x 4⅜"). NPG 5344; p.82 **Michael Ayrton**, (left) self-portrait, 1947. Pen and ink and wash, 384 x 305mm (15⅛ x 12"). © Estate of Michael Ayrton/National Portrait Gallery, London NPG 5537; (right) self-portrait, 1957–8. Oil and ripolin on board, 635 x 1268mm (25 x 50"). © Estate of Michael Ayrton/National Portrait Gallery, London NPG 6666; p.84 **Richard Hamilton**, self-portrait, 1970. Screen/collotype, 546 x 498mm (21½ x 19⅝"). © DACS. NPG 5278; p.85 **Henryk Gotlib**, self-portrait, *c*.1942. Painted plaster, height 630mm (24¾"). NPG 6642; p.86 (left) **Anne Killigrew**, published *c*.1683–1729. Isaac Beckett after a self-portrait published by John Smith, 240 x 190mm (9½ x 7½"). © Reserved. NPG D11896; (right) **Oriel Ross**, self-portrait, *c*.1928–31. Pen and ink, 357 x 256mm (14 x 10"). © Reserved. NPG 6578; p.87 **Mervyn Peake**, self-portrait, 1932. Oil on canvas, 600 x 505mm (23⅝ x 19⅞"). © By permission of David Higham Associates. Private collection, on loan to the National Portrait Gallery, London NPG L191.

Chapter eight

p.88 **Sir William Nicholson**, self-portrait based on a photograph of 1912. Woodcut, 110 x 83mm (4¼ x 3¼"). © Elizabeth Banks. NPG D695; p.90 **Gerald Scarfe**, self-portrait, 1988. Pen and Indian ink, 842 x 595mm (33⅛ x 23½"). © Gerald Scarfe. NPG 6431; p.91 **Susie Cooper**, self-portrait, *c*.1933. Ceramic mask, 314 x 159mm (12⅜ x 6¼"). Photograph © National Portrait Gallery, London NPG 6375; p.92 (above) **Isaac Oliver**, self-portrait, *c*.1590. Watercolour on vellum, 64 x 51mm (2½ x 2"). NPG 4852; (below) **Richard Cosway**, self-portrait, *c*.1790. Pencil and wash, 105 x 79mm (4⅛ x 3⅛"). NPG 304; p.93 **Thomas Gainsborough**, self-portrait, *c*.1758–9. Oil on canvas, 762 x 635mm (30 x 25"). NPG 4446; p.94 (left) **David Wilkie Wynfield**, self-portrait, 1860s. Albumen print, 213 x 162mm (8⅜ x 6⅜"). NPG P97; (right) **Oliver François Xavier Sarony**, self-portrait, late 1850s. Albumen print, 156 x 124mm (6⅛ x 4⅞"). NPG P613; p.95 **John Constable**, self-portrait, *c*.1799–1804. Pencil and black chalk heightened with white and red chalk, 248 x 194mm (9¾ x 7⅝"). NPG 901; p.96 **David Bomberg**, self-portrait, 1931. Charcoal and wash, 495 x 324mm (19½ x 12¾"). NPG 4821; p.97 **Frank Auerbach**, self-portrait, 1994–2001. Pencil and charcoal, 764 x 577mm (30⅛ x 22¾"). © Frank Auerbach/Marlborough Fine Art (London) Ltd/National Portrait Gallery, London NPG 6611; p.98 (left) **Oskar Kokoschka**, self-portrait, 1965. Lithograph, 987 x 654mm (38⅞ x 25¾"). © DACS 2005. NPG 5156; (right) **Leon Kossoff**, self-portrait, 1981. Oil on board, 424 x 330mm (16¾ x 13"). NPG 5772; p.99 **Dame Barbara Hepworth**, self-portrait, 1950. Oil and pencil on board, 305 x 267mm (12 x 10½"). © Alan Bowness, Hepworth estate. NPG 5919; p.100 **Lucian Freud**, self-portrait, 1963. Oil on canvas, 305 x 251mm (12 x 9⅞"). © The Artist; NPG 5205; p.101 **Gwen John**, self-portrait, *c*.1900. Oil on canvas, 610 x 378mm (24 x 14⅞"). © Estate of Gwen John 2005. All Rights Reserved, DACS. NPG 4439.

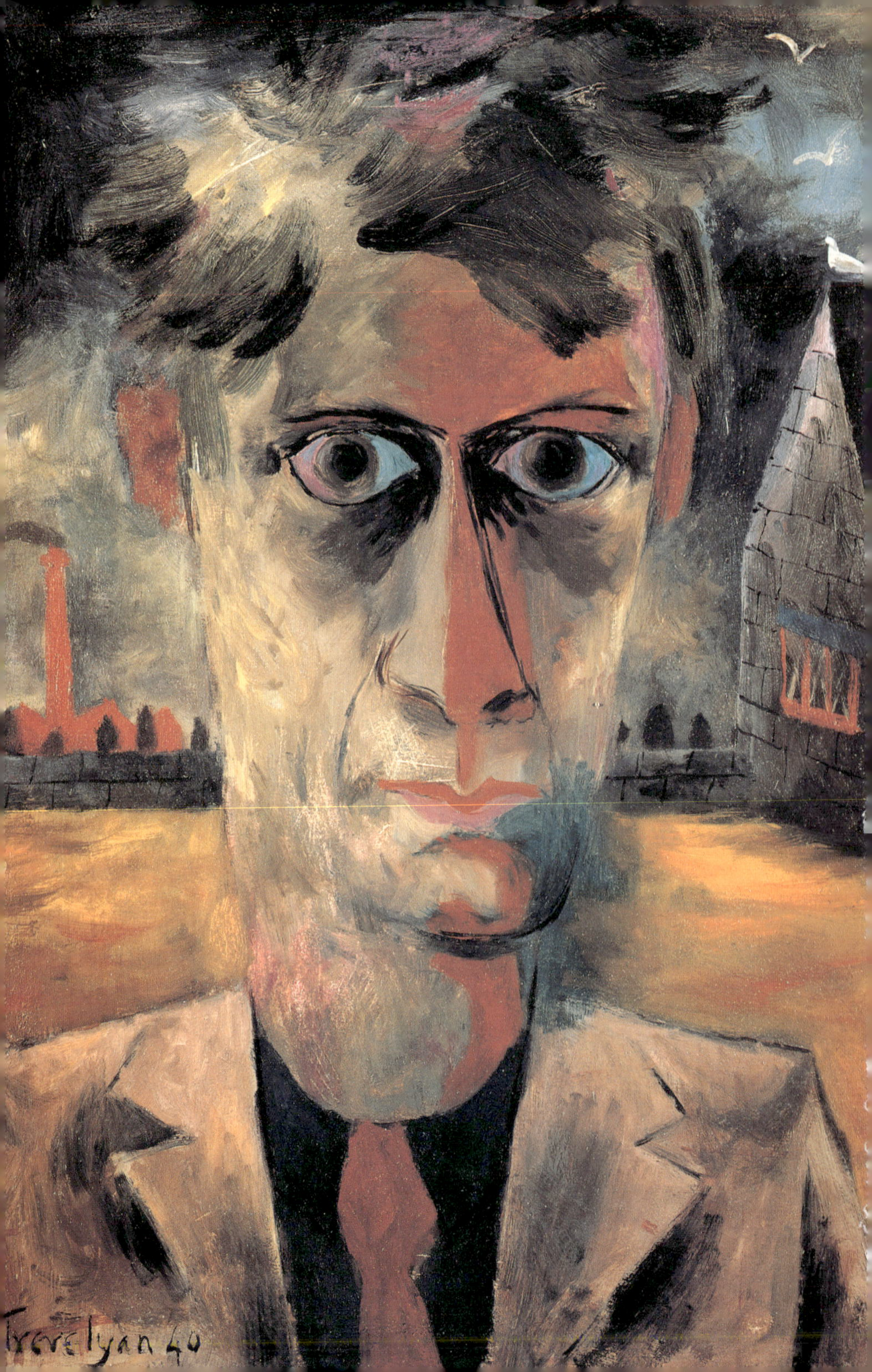

Trevelyan 40